COPENHAGEN STUDIES IN TRANSLATION

Vol. 2

WORDS THAT TEEM WITH MEENING
Copenhagen Views on Lexicography

COPENHAGEN STUDIES IN TRANSLATION

Vol. 2

Edited by

Jørgen Erik Nielsen

MUSEUM TUSCULANUM PRESS
University of Copenhagen 1992

© Museum Tusculanum Press 1992
Computer typeset by Kirsten Andersen, laserprinted
Printed in Denmark by Stougaard Jensen, Copenhagen
ISBN 87 7289 233 1
ISSN 0907 7901

Copenhagen Studies in Translation
General editors:
Cay Dollerup
Jørgen Erik Nielsen
Viggo Hjørnager Nielsen

The publication of this issue was supported by
The Faculty for the Humanities, University of Copenhagen

On the front cover: Samuel Johnson
Engraving by Alonzo Chappel based on a painting by Barry

MUSEUM TUSCULANUM PRESS
92, Njalsgade   DK–2300 Copenhagen S.

TABLE OF CONTENTS

Preface 3
Bent Nordhjem
    On the Use of Nominalised Phrasal Verbs
    in English Literary Prose 5
Henrik Gottlieb
    Idioms into English. Principles and Design
    of a Bilingual Dictionary of Current Idiomatic Usage 56
Jørgen Erik Nielsen
    Danish Dickens Translations as Sources of Neologisms
    in 19th-Century Dictionaries 82
Viggo Hjørnager Pedersen
    English Influence on Modern Danish Vocabulary and
    its Implications for Danish/English Lexicography 93
Jørgen Harrit
    Possession and Existence:
    a Problem in Active Danish-Russian Lexicography 115
Ellen M. Pedersen
    Synonymics after Chomsky: a Challenge in Progress 122
Arne Zettersten
    Tools for the Historical Linguist:
    Innovations in the use of English historical dictionaries,
    corpora and databases 131

PREFACE

The Center for Translation Studies and Lexicography at Copenhagen University functioned as a departmental unit from January 1989 till the end of 1991, when it was attached to the Department of English. Its activities have embraced both teaching and research, the latter comprising both practical lexicography and more theoretical work. At a meeting of the Center council in the autumn of 1990 it was decided to include among its publications a collection of essays by scholars attached to the Center or with a share in its work, and the outcome is the present volume.

In the opening article, Bent Nordhjem traces the development of nominalised verbal phrases in English and draws up a long list of NVP's with definitions of their meanings. The three following entries, by Henrik Gottlieb, Jørgen Erik Nielsen and Viggo Hjørnager Pedersen, are all concerned with aspects of contrastive approaches to English and Danish vocabulary, after which Jørgen Harrit takes up a problem for the lexicographer working on Danish and Russian. Ellen M. Pedersen then discusses the theoretical intricacies confronting one of the current projects of the Center: the compilation of a contrastive database of Danish-English synonyms. Arne Zettersten concludes the volume with a survey of historical English dictionaries and databases.

As is apparent, English dominates the scene, which reflects the fact that the majority of those attached to the Center have English as their subject. The volume contains one article about Russian, but the work done at the Center has embraced German, French and Greek lexicography too.

My thanks are due to Ms. Elisabeth Møller, who worked out an assessment of the manuscripts, recommending their publication, and to Ms. Kirsten Andersen, whose assistance in preparing the volume for the press has been extremely valuable.

Copenhagen, April 1992.   Jørgen Erik Nielsen

Bent Nordhjem

ON THE USE OF NOMINALISED PHRASAL VERBS IN ENGLISH LITERARY PROSE

Nominalised phrasal verbs in English

A nominalised phrasal verb - for short, an NPV - may be defined as a compound substantive consisting of the stem of a verb followed by an adverbial particle.

As in most other compound nouns, spellings vary. One finds, sometimes even in the same text, such different forms as *lookout*, *look-out*, and *look out*. For the purposes of this study I confess to a preference for the hyphenated forms, which make the structure of the nouns graphic.

The spelling difficulty reflects another difficulty. It is often impossible to tell whether one is faced by a verb-stem + a particle (ie a genuine NPV) or by a noun that happens to be postmodified by an adverb. Thus, when Laurence Sterne writes, 'Yorick replied, with a look up,' does he mean: with a look which was directed upwards (ie a noun + an adverb), or: while performing the act of looking up (ie a verb-stem + a particle, in other words a genuine NVP)? Given the inconsistencies of hyphenation the printed text cannot differentiate; nor is there always an audible difference in spoken English. (To avoid impossible decisions I have counted any possible NPV as an NPV in the statistical part of this study.)

The verbal stem which is the first component of an NPV is usually a monosyllable, as in *break-in*, *run-away*, although it may occasionally be a trochaic disyllable, as in *cover-up*, *follow-through*. NPVs with a disyllabic verb-stem are comparative newcomers: In the corpus of literary prose on which this study is based, they occur only after 1920.

The category of particles capable of entering into NPVs is small but vague. It may be defined as consisting of short adverbs, never ending in *-ly*, mainly monosyllabic or disyllabic, and denoting locality or movement (literally as well as figuratively). Natural candidates are: *about, around, away, back, between, by, down, in, off, out, over, past, round, to, up, and on, through, together*. In my material the first 15 occur in NPVs both before and after 1920, the last three - evidently a recent development - only after 1920.

As the term suggests, an NPV is structurally like (has the composition of) a phrasal verb; and in fact most NPVs are related to phrasal verbs. This is the case whenever there exists a phrasal verb with the same components and with a meaning from which that of the corresponding noun may be naturally inferred, eg *break down, hand out, make up.* In most cases, however, the noun has a more specialised meaning than the verb; and in not a few cases the meaning of an NPV cannot be deduced from any phrasal verb, eg *drawback, lay-by, lean-to.* This makes it misleading to define an NPV simply as a phrasal verb converted into a noun; it seems preferable to define it as a noun composed of a verbal stem followed by a particle.

The ease with which verb-stem and particle join to form a noun is one of the striking features of modern English. In this respect, the English language contrasts interestingly with other Germanic languages, which cannot perform the same trick with the same ease. It is by no means impossible to compile a list of Danish NPVs comparable to the English ones we are discussing, eg *hugaf, lukaf, komsammen, kørom, rodsammen, rykind, skrabsammen, skrabud, skældud, spilopper, svingom*. But the fact remains that it is not a productive type of noun-formation in Danish. On the other hand, Danish, like other Germanic languages but unlike English, is highly productive in another type of noun-formation, where particle + verb-stem + suffix join to form a substantive, eg *build-up* vs *opbygning*, *opbyggelse*. It seems natural to connect the flexibility of English when it comes to forming nouns from the stems of verbs (simple as well as phrasal) with the fact that the English verb-stem is morphologically neutral; it may be an imperative, an infinitive, a present-tense form (though not in the third person singular), occasionally even a past tense and a past participle, whereas in other Germanic languages a verb-stem primarily suggests the imperative mood.

English also admits compound nouns consisting of verb-stem + noun (eg *pickpocket, scarecrow, spoilsport*) but not as freely as compounds made up of verb-stem + particle. In this respect English contrasts interestingly with French, which is rich in compound nouns consisting of verb + noun (eg *casse-cou, couvre-feu, presse-citron*), while it has few compounds consisting of verb + adverb (eg *passe-partout*). Important reasons for this difference between English and French may be (1) that French is poor in monosyllabic particles, and (2) that French does not admit compounds in which the first component is the object of the second component (cf *book-lover* vs *amateur de livres*).

In English the same combination of words sometimes occurs both as a phrasal verb, an adjectivised phrasal verb, and a nominalised phrasal verb, eg *my boots lace up, lace-up boots, lace-ups*. Adjectivised phrasal verbs are not always easy to distinguish from nominalised phrasal verbs which are used to premodify other nouns, as in *fall-out shelter, make-up artist*. Such occurrences of NPVs, which all seem to be recent, are not counted in the statistical part of the present study.

The history of NPVs in English literary prose
In the following pages I shall try to sketch the outline of the history of NPVs in English literary prose since 1726 on the basis of a selection of such prose works.

I shall make no attempt to estimate the total number of NPVs existing in any given period. Such estimates, which have been undertaken before, can never be more than approximative (see Notes).

The same, however, is true of what I am attempting here: to gauge the acceptability or normality, as it were the literary respectability, of NPVs as a class and as individual words in different periods and with different writers. As the works examined here can be no more than samples, and as oversights are only too likely, this study cannot hope to achieve anything like accuracy. Still, with its inevitable shortcomings, it does seem to warrant some historical generalisations.

My NPV count begins a little more than two and a half centuries ago with Swift's *Gulliver's Travels* (1726). (It has to start somewhere, and although NPVs date back to Middle English, the odds against coming across any NPV in any literary prose work before Swift are discouraging).

My material suggests a division of the literature examined into three periods: (1) 1726-1813, (2) 1814-1920, and (3) after 1920. The investigation which follows will show a quite unmistakable development: from no use or hardly any use of NPVs to a quite extensive use of them. And the transitions from period 1 to period 2, and from 2 to 3, seem rather marked.

In the following chronological surveys each title is preceded by the year of publication (in the case of Jane Austen's *Lady Susan*, the supposed years of composition). Each title is followed by one or two figures: the first figure indicates the number of different NPVs observed in the text; the second figure (which is bracketed and only supplied where it differs from the first) indicates the total number of NPVs, identical or different, found in the text.

The quotations given under the book-titles are from the editions listed at the end of this article. The text is quoted as found, with the following reservations:

All quotations are reproduced with an initial capital.

---: three dashes indicate gaps in a quotation where scattered passages have been brought together to provide the necessary context for the NPV.

'-': quotation marks are used round passages which in the source are marked as reported speech. (However, in the original the quotation marks may surround a longer passage than the one which is quoted).

Each quotation is identified with a dual reference: (1) book, volume, part, etc (only where necessary and always in Roman numerals) + chapter number or heading; and (2) the page on which the headword occurs.

[-] : square brackets are used round a reference without a quotation. (Quotations are omitted in some cases where the context reveals nothing that has not been adequately illustrated by earlier quotations).

Period 1: 1726-1813. Chronological survey of works
1726 Jonathan Swift, *Gulliver's Travels*: 0
1749 Henry Fielding, *Tom Jones*: 1
    LOOK-OUT: As the Captain was always on the Look-out, no Glance, Gesture, or Word escaped him (I,II: 52).
1759 Samuel Johnson, *The History of Rasselas*: 0
1759-67 Laurence Sterne, *Tristram Shandy*: 2
    DRAWBACK: So that not withstanding my father had the happiness of reading the oddest books in the universe, and had moreover, in himself, the oddest way of thinking, that ever man in it was bless'd

with, yet it had this drawback upon him after all, - that it laid him open to some of the oddest and most whimsical distresses (III,30: 157).

LOOK-UP: Yorick replied, with a look up, and a gentle squeeze of Eugenius's hand, and that was all (I,12: 21).

1768 Laurence Sterne, *A Sentimental Journey*: 0
1778 Fanny Burney, *Evelina*: 2

RUNAWAY: 'Oh ho, my little runaway, have I found you at last? I have been scampering all over the gardens for you' (II,25: 200).

TAKE-IN: 'I thought, at the time,' said Mr Branghton, 'that three shillings was an exorbitant price for a place in the gallery --- I find it's as arrant a take-in as ever I met with' (I,21: 91).

1793-94 Jane Austen, *Lady Susan*: 0
1796 Matthew Lewis, *The Monk*: 0
1811 Jane Austen, *Sense and Sensibility*: 1

DRAWBACK: 'It will be all to one a better match for your sister. Two thousand a year without debt or drawback - except the little love-child, indeed' (30: 207)

1813 Jane Austen, *Pride and Prejudice*: 1

SET DOWN: 'I wish you had been there, my dear, to have given him one of your set downs, I quite detest the man' (3: 61)

It will be observed that only 5 of the 10 works sampled in period 1 (2 of them exceptionally long) contain NPVs; 3 of them contain only 1 each, and 2 of them 2 each. Although it is possible that the works examined are not entirely representative, it seems a safe enough generalisation that NPVs are few and far between in the literary prose of the period 1726-1813.

Period 2: 1814-1920. Chronological survey of works
1814 Jane Austen, *Mansfield Park*: 4 (12)

BREAK-UP: He could not have devised any thing more likely to raise his consequence than this week's absence, occurring as it did at the very time of her brother's going away, of William Price's going too, and completing the sort of general break-up of a party which had been so animated (29: 290).

DRAWBACK: She began to feel that when her own release from Portsmouth came, her happiness would have a material drawback in leaving Susan behind (43: 409). To be finding herself, perhaps, within three days, transported to Mansfield, was an image of the greatest felicity - but it would have been a material drawback, to be owing such felicity to persons in whose feelings and conduct, at the present moment, she saw so much to condemn (45: 425). Their own inclinations ascertained, there were no difficulties behind, no drawbacks of poverty or parent (48: 455). [Also 8: 106; 27: 269 (twice); 34: 335; 37: 365; 39: 381.]

LOOK OUT: Mr Price was only calling out, 'Come girls - come, Fan - come, Sue - take care of yourselves - keep a sharp look out' (41: 396).

TAKE IN: 'I know so many who have married in the full expectation and confidence of some one particular advantage in the connection, or accomplishment or good quality in the person, who have found themselves entirely deceived, and been obliged to put up with exactly the reverse! What is this, but a take in?' (5: 79).

1816 Jane Austen, *Emma*: 6 (11)

CRY-OUT: 'The advantage of the match I felt to be all on her side; and had not the smallest doubt (nor have I now) that there would be a general cry-out upon her extreme good luck' (8: 88).

DRAWBACK: 'If I did not know her to be happy now,' said Emma, seriously, 'which, in spite of every little drawback from her scrupulous conscience, she must be, I could not bear these thanks' (48: 408). [Also 19: 175; 20: 178; 23: 205; 32: 277.]

LOOK-OUT: 'One cannot creep upon a journey; one cannot help

11

getting on faster than one has planned; and the pleasure of coming in upon one's friends before the look-out begins, is worth a great deal more than any little exertion it needs' (23: 203). 'I shall write to Mrs Partridge in a day or two, and shall give her a strict charge to be on the look-out for any thing eligible' (35: 300).

PUT-OFF: 'She thinks there will be another put-off. She does not depend upon his coming as much as I do' (14: 140).

SET OUT: 'When you are tired of eating strawberries in the garden, there shall be cold meat in the house.' 'Well - as you please; only don't have a great set out' (42: 351).

WIND-UP: All the grandeur of the connection seemed dependent on the elder sister, who was *very well married*, to a gentleman in a *great way*, near Bristol, who kept two carriages! That was the wind-up of the history; that was the glory of Miss Hawkins (22: 196).

1818 Jane Austen, *Persuasion*: 2

BREAK-UP: Lady Russell felt this break-up of the family exceedingly (5: 63).

SET-TO: 'We had a famous set-to at rat-hunting all the morning, in my father's great barns' (22: 224).

1836-37 Charles Dickens, *The Pickwick Papers*: 7 (8)

BREAK DOWN: 'Discover - nonsense - too much shaken by the break down - besides - extreme caution - gave up the post-chaise - walked on - took a hackney coach -' (10 : 201)

DRAWBACK: 'There was only one drawback to the beauty of the whole picture' (14: 262). 'I don't know better company anywhere; but he has that one drawback. If the ghost of his grandfather, sir, was to rise before him this minute, he'd ask him for the loan of his acceptance on an eighteen-penny stamp' (44: 713).

KNOCK DOWN: 'There are some funny dogs among us, and they will have their joke, you know; but you mustn't mind them.' 'I'll try and bear up agin such a reg'lar knock down o' talent,' replied Sam

(37: 610).

LOOK-OUT: 'Looking at Whitehall, sir? - fine place - little window - somebody else's head off there, eh, sir? - he didn't keep a sharp look-out enough either, - eh, sir, eh?' (2: 79).

PULL-UP: '"Except of me Mary my dear as your walentine and think over what I've said. - My dear Mary I will now conclude." That's all,' said Sam. 'That's rather a sudden pull up, ain't it, Sammy?' inquired Mr Weller (33: 542).

SET OUT: He called his companion's attention to the large gilt button which displayed a bust of Mr Pickwick in the centre, and the letters 'P.C.' on either side. 'P.C.' said the stranger, -'queer set out - old fellow's likeness, and "P.C."' (2: 87).

TURN-OUT: 'I wonder what all the people we pass, can see in us to make them stare so.' 'It's a neat turn-out,' replied Ben Allen, with something of pride in his tone (50: 795).

1845 Benjamin Disraeli, *Sybil*: 4 (8)

BLOWOUT: 'I wonder what the nobs has for supper,' said the young one pensively. 'Lots of kidneys I dare say.' 'Oh! no; sweets is the time of day in these here blowouts' (V,7: 380). 'If we only get our rights, won't we have a blow out!' (VI,3: 422).

START-UP: 'Your lordship can speak to me without reserve, and I am used to these start-ups. It is part of the trade; but an old soldier is not to be deceived by such feints' (IV,13: 325).

STICK-OUT: 'I've been at play, sir, several times in forty years, and have seen as great stick-outs as ever happened in this country' (III,1: 182). Good Mrs Carey still gossips with her neighbours round her well-stored stall, and tells wonderful stories of the great stick-out and riots of -42 (VI,13: 496).

TURN OUT: 'Brethren, is it your pleasure that there shall be a turn out for ten days at Claughton and Hicks?' (IV,4: 269). 'I have seen a many things in my time,' said Mr Trotman; 'some risings and some strikes, and as stiff turn-outs as may be' (VI,3: 423). [Also VI,1: 411.]

1847 Benjamin Disraeli, *Tancred*: 1 (2)

PASSOVER: 'We know that, even in the time of Jesus, Hebrews came up to Jerusalem at the Passover from every province of the Roman Empire' (III,4: 258). 'You will not let them persecute us, as they did a few years back, because they said we crucified their children at the feast of our passover?' (V,7: 537).

1847 Charlotte Brontë, *Jane Eyre*: 3 (4)

BLOW-UP: 'Oh, gracious, mamma! Spare us the enumeration! *Aureste*, we all know them: danger of bad example to innocence of childhood; distractions and consequent neglect of duty on the part of the attached - mutual alliance and reliance; confidence thence resulting - insolence accompanying - mutiny and general blow-up' (17: 207).

CASTAWAY: 'It becomes my duty to warn you that this girl, who might be one of God's own lambs, is a little castaway - not a member of the true flock, but evidently an interloper and an alien' (7: 98). [Also 35: 440.]

LOOKOUT: I was forgetting all his faults, for which I had once kept a sharp lookout (18: 217).

1847-48 William Thackeray, *Vanity Fair*: 7 (17)

CASTAWAY: What an utter castaway she must have thought her son-in-law for permitting such a godless diversion! (45: 527). 'I have been wandering ever since then - a poor castaway, scorned for being miserable, and insulted because I am alone' (66: 775).

DRAWBACK: Amongst these would-be fugitives, Jos remarked the Lady Bareacres and her daughter, who sate in their carriage in the *porte-cochère* of their hotel, all their imperials packed, and the only drawback to whose flight was the same want of motive power which kept Jos stationary (32: 375).

GO-BY: Being made an honest woman of, so to speak, Becky would not consort any longer with these dubious ones, and cut Lady Crackenbury when the latter nodded to her from her opera-box; and gave Mrs Washington White the go-by in the Ring (48: 560).

LOOK-OUT: He too wanted to fly, and was on the look-out for the means of escape (32: 376). 'And I'll go and see her to-morrow?' Miss Osborne asked. 'That's your look-out. She don't come in here, mind' (50: 579). [Also 'Before the Curtain': 33; 6: 97; 14: 183; 25: 304; 52: 610; 67: 791.]

SET-OFF: Through the interest of my Lord Bareacres, and as a set-off for the dinner at the restaurateur's, George got a card for Captain and Mrs Osborne; which circumstance greatly elated him (29: 341).

TUCK-OUT: Old Dobbin, his father, who now respected him for the first time, gave him two guineas publicly; most of which he spent in a general tuck-out for the school (5: 84).

TURN-OUT: Mrs Joseph Sedley's servant --- and Mr Osborne's man agreed, as they followed George and William into the church, that it was a 'reg'lar shabby turn-hout; and with scarce so much as a breakfast or a wedding favour' (22: 259). But there was no such swell in Calcutta as Waterloo Sedley, I have heard say: and he had the handsomest turn-out, gave the best bachelor dinners, and had the finest plate in the whole place (59: 685). The bugles were sounding the turn-out and the drums beating in the various quarters of the town (30: 348).

1849 Charlotte Brontë, *Shirley*: 1

DRAWBACK: One slight drawback there was - where is the friendship without it? - Sir Philip had a literary turn (27: 446).

1849-50 Charles Dickens, *David Copperfield*: 3 (8)

DRAWBACK: 'It's one of the drawbacks of our line of business' (30: 440). [Also 7: 97; 24: 362.]

LOOKOUT: 'Mr. Peggotty and myself will constantly keep a double lookout together on our goods and chattels' (57: 809). 'The probability is, all will be found so exciting, alow and aloft, that when the lookout, stationed in the main-top, cries Land-ho! we shall be very considerably astonished!' (57: 812). [Also 13: 187; 13: 202.]

SET-OFF: I heard that one boy, who was a coal-merchant's son, came as a set-off against the coal-bill, and was called on that account 'Exchange or Barter' (6: 92).

1851-53 Elizabeth Gaskell, *Cranford*: 3

GO-BETWEEN: 'You must have played your cards badly, my little Matty, somehow or another - wanted your brother to be a good go-between, eh! little one?' (16: 213).

LOOK AROUND: Miss Matty started into wakefulness, with a strange, bewildered look around, as if we were not the people she expected to see about her (5: 84).

THROW-BACK: He had a wiry, well-trained, elastic figure; a stiff military throw-back of his head, and a springing step (1: 44).

1854 Charles Dickens, *Hard Times*: 3 (7)

LOOK-OUT: 'I shall be on the look-out for you, when you come back' (I,16: 143). 'I also told you, if you remember, that I was up to the gold spoon look-out' (II,5: 182). Mrs Sparsit, lying by to recover the tone of her nerves in Mr Bounderby's retreat, kept such a sharp look-out, night and day, under her Coriolanian eyebrows, that her eyes, like a couple of lighthouses on an iron-bound coast, might have warned all prudent mariners from that bold rock her Roman nose and the dark and craggy region in its neighbourhood (II,9: 218). 'Never you mind what I took her for; that's my look-out' (III,3: 264). [Also III,7: 296.]

SET-OUT: 'She must just hate and detest the whole set-out of us' (I,8: 91).

SHAKE-DOWN: 'I told him I would give her a shake-down here, last night' (I,7: 85).

1854-55 Elizabeth Gaskell, *North and South*: 6 (20)
>CASTAWAY: 'A castaway, lonely as Robinson Crusoe' (20: 218).
>DRAWBACK: 'I suffered too much myself; not that I was not extremely happy with the poor dear general, - but still disparity of age is a drawback' (1: 36). [Also 1: 44; 2: 49; 51: 524.]
>LOOK-OUT: The yard, too, with the great doors in the dead wall as a boundary, was but a dismal look-out for the sitting-rooms of the house (15: 158). 'I am on the lookout for a situation in Milton' (51: 524). [Also 20: 213.]
>PULL-UP: All his business plans had received a check, a sudden pull-up from this approaching turn-out (18: 196).
>PUSH AWAY: Once or twice she came up to kiss him; and he submitted to it, giving her a little push away when she had done (30: 317).
>TURN-OUT: 'Arter all, his bark's waur than his bite, and yo' may tell him one o' his turn-outs said so, if yo' like' (19: 203). 'It was only the last time Mr Thornton was here that he said, those were no true friends who helped to prolong the struggle by assisting the turn-outs. And this Boucher-man was a turn-out, was he not?' (20: 211). One or two thought Thornton looked out of spirits; and, of course, he must lose by this turn-out (20: 217). [Also 15: 170; 18: 194; 18: 196; 20: 218; 36: 365 (twice).]

1855-57 Charles Dickens, *Little Dorrit* 7 (9)
>CASTAWAY: 'Will you be able to have no affection for him when he is gone, poor castaway, gone?' (I,19: 273).
>CUTAWAY: Sometimes these correspondents assumed facetious names, as the Brick, Bellows, Old Gooseberry, Wideawake, Snooks, Mops, Cutaway, the Dogs-meat Man (I,6: 106).
>DRAWBACK: 'The only thing that stands in its way, sir, is the Credit.' This drawback, rather severely felt by most people who engaged in commercial transactions with the inhabitants of Bleeding

Heart Yard, was a large stumbling-block in Mrs Plornish's trade (II,13: 632).
GO-BETWEEN: There was a string of people already straggling in, whom it was not difficult to identify as the nondescript messengers, go-betweens, and errand-bearers of the place (I,9: 131).
LOOK OUT: If the ship went down with them yet sticking to it, that was the ship's look out, and not theirs (I,10: 163). 'I have not had so pleasant a greeting --- since we last walked to and fro, looking down at the Mediterranean.' 'Ah!' returned Mr Meagles. 'Something like a look out, *that* was, wasn't it?'
(I,16: 236).
SET-OFF: Thus was she always balancing her bargains with the Majesty of heaven, posting up the entries to her credit, strictly keeping her set-off, and claiming her due (I,5: 89).
TURN OUT: Mr Tip hired a cabriolet, horse, and groom, a very neat turn out, which was usually to be observed for two or three hours at a time gracing the Borough High Street (I,36: 474). Bright the carriage looked, sleek the horses looked, gleaming the harness looked, luscious and lasting the liveries looked. A rich, responsible turn-out (II,16: 672).

1855 Anthony Trollope; *The Warden*: 1
    LOOK OUT: He had not told Eleanor when he would return, but she was on the look out for him by every train by which he could arrive (19: 256).

1857 Anthony Trollope; *Barchester Towers*: 5 (8)
    BREAK-UP: 'Your going will be a great break-up to our party' (II,11: 279).
    CASTAWAY: 'You might let her hear from your consecrated lips that she is not a castaway because she is a Roman' (I,11: 88).
    DRAWBACK: 'A ready-made family is a drawback' (I,15: 123). Two little drawbacks to the general happiness did take place, but they

were of a temporary nature, and apparent rather than real. The first was the downfall of young Harry Greenacre, and the other the uprise of Mrs Lookaloft and her family (III,5: 372). [Also II,13: 297; III,3: 357.]

LOOK-OUT: If a man gave him credit, that was the man's look-out; Bertie Stanhope troubled himself nothing further (III,8: 400).

TAKE-IN: 'I got a ton and a half at Bradley's in the High Street,' said the archdeacon, 'and it was a complete take-in. I don't believe there was five hundred-weight of guano in it' (II,4: 209).

1858 Anthony Trollope; *Doctor Thorne*: 5 (10)

CASTAWAY: Frank had loved her so truly when she was so poor, such an utter castaway (47: 610).

DRAWBACK: 'Rank, however, has its drawbacks, Miss Thorne, as well as its privileges.' 'I should not object to the drawbacks,' said the doctor's niece, 'presuming them to be of some use' (4: 66). [Also 4:68; 6: 87 (twice); 47: 623.]

GET-UP: He was a man much addicted to hunting, as far as the get-up of the thing was concerned; he was great in boots and breeches (5: 80).

GO-BETWEEN: 'I find that, in spite of what has occurred, the closest intimacy exists between the two families; that poor Beatrice, who is so very young, and not so prudent as she should be, is made to act as a go-between' (27: 360).

LOOKOUT: 'That's my lookout' (10: 145)

1860 Wilkie Collins: *The Woman in White*: 3 (6)

BREAK-UP: 'Before they had been quite four months in our neighbourhood there was a dreadful scandal and a miserable break-up in their household' (III. The Story Continued by Walter Hartright, 7: 487).

DRAWBACK: 'I can match you at chess, backgammon, écarté, and (with the inevitable female drawbacks) even at billiards as well' (I.

The Story Begun by Walter Hartright, 5: 61). [Also II. The Story Continued by Eliza Michelson, 1: 388; III. The Story Continued by Mrs Catherick: 558.]

LOOK-OUT: Those two men had been placed on the look-out near the church in anticipation of my appearance at Old Welmingham (III. The Story Continued by Walter Hartright, 9: 516). [Also III. The Story Continued by Walter Hartright, 1: 562.]

1860-61 Charles Dickens, *Great Expectations*: 7 (13)

DRAWBACK: Nor was there any drawback on my little turret bedroom, beyond there being such a very thin ceiling between me and the flagstaff (25: 232). [Also 7: 77.]

KICK-UP: Upon which he put down his head, blew a cloud of smoke out of his nose, and vanished with a kick-up of his hind-legs and a florish of his tail (3: 48).

LOCK-UP: 'And warn't it me as had been tried afore, and as had been know'd up hill and down dale in Bridewells and Lock-Ups?' (42: 365).

LOOK OUT: Nor did the counting-house where Herbert assisted, show in my eyes as at all a good Observatory; being a back second floor up a yard, of a grimy presence in all particulars, and with a look into another back second floor, rather than a look out (22; 209). The galley was kept steady, and the silent eager look-out at the water was resumed (54: 455). [Also 22: 200; 24: 224; 54: 455.]

RUNAWAY: 'Convicts! Runaways! Guard! This way for the runaway convicts!' (5: 66).

SHAKE-DOWN: He considered the chambers and his own lodging as temporary residences, and advised me to look out at once for a 'fashionable crib' near Hyde Park, in which he could have 'a shake-down' (41: 359).

TOSS-UP: 'As to the result, it's a toss-up. I told you from the first it was a toss-up' (20: 191). 'It would be chance work to give an opinion how a fellow of that sort will turn out in such circumstances, because it's a toss-up between two results' (48: 402).

1866 George Eliot, *Felix Holt, the Radical*: 4 (7)

GET-UP: The vision of the graceful well-appointed Mr Christian, who sneered at Scales about his 'get-up', having to walk back to the house with only one tail to his coat, was a source of so much enjoyment to the butler, that the fair Cherry began to be quite jealous of the joke (12: 234).

GO-OFF: 'You're none of a Tory, eh, sir? You won't go to vote for Debarry? That was what I said at the very first go-off' (11: 220).

LOOKOUT: Beyond the village several small boys were stationed on the lookout (1: 85). [Also 1: 103; 28: 376; 43: 529].

MAKE UP: What the farce wanted in costume or 'make up' it gained in the reality of the mortification which excited the general laughter (12: 234).

1868 Wilkie Collins; *The Moonstone*: 8 (16)

BREAK-DOWN: Here was another of your average good Christians, and here was the usual break-down, consequent on that same average Christianity being pushed too far! (First Period, 23: 181).

CASTAWAY: [First Narrative, 1: 193; First Narrative, 6: 229.]

DRAWBACK: Bating her lame foot and her leanness (this last a horrid drawback to a woman, in my opinion), the girl had some pleasing qualities in the eyes of a man (First Period, 23: 179). [Also First Period, 6: 46; First Narrative, 7: 246; Second Narrative, 2: 262; Third Narrative, 1: 278.]

GO-BETWEEN: 'No young lady in Miss Verinder's position could manage such a risky matter as that by herself. A go-between she must have, and who so fit, I ask again, as Rosanna Spearman?' (First Period, 21: 167).

LOOK-OUT: 'I had better not invite the girl's confidence, with the Sergeant on the look-out to surprise us together' (First Period, 17:

147). [Also Third Narrative, 8: 338 (twice); Third Narrative, 9: 358.]

LOOK UP: She put the question with a sudden flash in her eyes, and a sudden look up into Mr. Godfrey's face (First Narrative, 2: 202).

SET-DOWN: 'In all my experience along the dirtiest ways of this dirty little world, I have never met with such a thing as a trifle yet.' --- Mr. Superintendent - taking his set-down rather sulkily - asked if he should summon the women (First Period, 12: 102).

SHAKE UP: How the Monday affected the rest of the household I don't know. The Monday gave *me* a good shake up (First Period, 23: 179).

1871-72 George Eliot, *Middlemarch*: 4 (5)

LOOK-OUT: Lord Medlicote's man was on the look-out for just such a horse (23: 272). [Also 64: 706.]

PULL-UP: Some years after his marriage he told Mary that his happiness was half owing to Farebrother, who gave him a strong pull-up at the right moment (Finale: 891).

SET-OFF: He was much obliged to Casaubon in the past, but really the act of marrying this wife was a set-off against the obligation (37: 395).

TOSS UP: 'It is a mere toss up whether I shall ever do more than keep myself decently' (83: 869).

1877 Henry James, *The American*: 4

COME-DOWN: 'Three or four Bellegardes, in the seventeenth and eighteenth centuries, took wives out of the *bourgeoisie* - accepted lawyers' daughters.' 'A lawyer's daughter - that's a come-down?' (8: 136).

FALL-OFF: 'Oh come,' Newman protested; 'I'm not an honest barbarian either, by a good deal. I'm a great fall-off from *him*' (3: 40).

GADABOUT: 'Since then I've seen no more Americans. I think my daughter-in-law has; she's a great gadabout; she sees every one' (10:

162).

WIND-UP: 'You might have done something more to the purpose. It's about the meanest wind-up of a man's legitimate business I can imagine!' (19: 345).

1878 Henry James, *Daisy Miller*: 0
1881 Henry James, *The Portrait of a Lady*: 4 (8)

BREAK-UP: He had kept, evidently in spite of shocks, every one of his merits - properties these partaking of the essence of great decent houses, as one might put it; resembling their innermost fixtures and ornaments, not subject to vulgar shifting and removable only by some whole break-up (27: 247).

DRAWBACK: Society, moreover, had no drawacks for her; she liked even the tiresome parts (40: 342). [Also 24: 221 (twice); 39: 336; 51: 447.]

LOOKOUT: Everything he did was *pose - pose* so subtly considered that if one were not on the lookout one mistook it for impulse (39: 331).

SET-OFF: He had evidently taken Henrietta's affairs much to heart, and believed that he owed her a set-off to this illusory visit to Bedfordshire (20: 178).

1886 Henry James, *The Bostonians*: 3

DRAWBACK: She had the advantages as well as the drawbacks of a nervous organization (3: 18).

LOOK-OUT: He didn't trouble himself much to ask what had saved him; whatever it was it had produced a reaction, so that he felt rather ashamed of having found his look-out of late so blank (22: 180).

STAND-BY: Her mother liked to think that she was quick and graceful, and she questioned her exhaustively as to the progress of this interesting episode; she didn't see why, as she said, it shouldn't be a permanent 'stand-by' for Verena (13: 86).

1886 Thomas Hardy, *The Mayor of Casterbridge*: 2

TUCK-IN: 'Come to my house and we will have a solid, staunch tuck-in' (9: 68).

WIND-UP: 'As a wind-up to the Royal visit the hit [ie a 'skimmington-ride'] will be all the more pat by reason of their great elevation today' (37: 269).

1888 Edward Bellamy, *Looking Backward, 2000-1887*: 4

BREAKDOWN: These exchanges money effected - how equitably, might be seen in a walk from the tenement-house districts to the Back Bay - at the cost of an army of men taken from productive labor to manage it, with constant ruinous breakdowns of its machinery, and a general debauching influence on mankind (28: 223).

KNOCKDOWN: 'I was a little apprehensive at one time that I should undergo what I believe you used to call a knockdown in the nineteenth century, if I did not act rather promptly. I remembered that the Bostonians of your day were famous pugilists' (4: 56).

LOCKOUT: There was in it, as in all the newspapers of that date, a great deal about the labor troubles, strikes, lockouts, boycotts, the programmes of the labor parties, and the wild threats of the anarchists (24: 182).

SET-OFF: 'Not only justice but civility is enforced by our judges in all sorts of intercourse. No value of service is accepted as a set-off to boorish or offensive manners' (19: 155).

1888 Henry James, *The Aspern Papers*: 0
1889 Mark Twain, *A Connecticut Yankee at King Arthur's Court*: 8 (11)

BLOW-OUT: All of a sudden here comes along a man who slashes out nearly four dollars on a single blow-out; and not only that, but acts as if it made him tired to handle such small sums (32: 297).

GIVEAWAY: 'The stock was for sale at a giveaway' (42: 379).

LAY-OUT: There was a very good lay-out for the king's-evil business - very tidy and creditable. The king sat under a canopy of state, about him were clustered a large body of the clergy in full canonicals (26: 241). No, if anybody wants to make his living exhibiting a king as a peasant, let him take the layout; I can do better with a menagerie, and last longer (27: 254). 'And so we'll shop around and get up this layout, now, and don't you worry about the expense' (31: 286).

LOOK-OUT: I kept a sharp look-out (36: 338). I picketed the great embankments thrown up around our lines by the dynamite explosion - merely a look-out of a couple of boys to announce the enemy when he should appear again (43: 397)

MAKE-UP: The circus man paid no attention to her; didn't even seem to see her. And she - she was no more startled at his fantastic make-up than if she was used to his like every day of her life (1: 41).

ROUND-UP: Young Barker the bellows-mender is home again, and looks much improved by his vacation round-up among the out-lying smithies (26: 248).

SEND-OFF: Everybody knows and likes The Bess, everybody knows and likes Sir Sag.; come, let us give the lads a good send-off (39: 354).

SHAKE-DOWN: The man was still asleep, on a straw shake-down, on the clay floor (30: 275).

1890 William Morris, *News from Nowhere*: 6 (8)

BREAKDOWN: Yet one ally they had, and that was the rapidly approaching breakdown of the whole system founded on the World-Market and its supply (17: 102).

BREAK-UP: 'As to the big murky places which were once, as we know, the centres of manufacture, they have, like the brick and mortar desert of London, disappeared; --- some approach to their break-up as centres would probably have taken place, even if we had not changed our habits so much' (10: 58). 'The entire break-up of all society would have followed' (17: 107).

DRAWBACK: 'A great many people live there,' said he, 'as, with all drawbacks, it is a pleasant place' (24: 139). [Also 14: 76.]

LEAN-TO: On the other, the south side, of the road was an octagonal building with a high roof, not unlike the Baptistry at Florence in outline, except that it was surrounded by a lean-to that clearly made an arcade or cloisters to it (4: 19).

LOCK-OUT: 'Do you mean actual fighting with weapons?' said I, 'or the strikes and lock-outs and starvation of which we have heard?' (17: 89).

LOOK-OUT: 'There is George Brightling on the look-out for a stroke of work' (2: 9).

1890 Rudyard Kipling, *Plain Tales from the Hills*: 6 (8)

DRAWBACK: Ethnologically and politically the notion was correct. The only drawback was that it was altogether wrong ('Tods' Amendment': 181). [Also 'His Wedded Wife': 155.]

LOOK-OUT: 'I'm a Freelance up here on leave, on the look-out for what I can loot' ('Consequences': 113).

MAKE-UP: Janoo sat down composedly on one of his beds to discuss the probabilities of the whole thing being a *bunao*, or 'make-up' ('In the House of Suddhoo': 148). 'I hadn't the heart to part with my old make-ups when I married. Will this do?' There was a loathly *fakir* salaaming in the doorway ('The Bronckhorst Divorce-Case': 216).

MARCH-PAST: A march-past concluded the campaign ('The Rout of the White Hussars': 207).

THROW-BACK: Most men and all women know the spasm. It only lasts for three breaths as a rule, must be a 'throw-back' to times when men and women were rather worse than they are now ('The Bronckhorst Divorce-Case': 215).

TURN-OUT: The turn-out of Miss Youghal's Arab was a wonder and a delight ('Miss Youghal's *Sais*': 53).

1891 Thomas Hardy, *Tess of the d'Urbervilles*: 4

CASTAWAY: 'Who cares about the looks of a castaway like me?' (44: 251).

KICK-UP: She did not abhor dancing, but she was not going to dance here. --- A couple had fallen, and lay in a mixed heap. --- 'My good Lord, what a kick-up they are having there!' (10: 55).

LOOK ROUND: 'Then we'll have another look round' (52: 300).

TURN-OUT: The second vehicle was not a humble conveyance like the first, but a spick-and-span gig or dog-cart, highly varnished and equipped. --- The muslined form of Tess could be seen standing still, undecided, beside this turn-out, whose owner was talking to her (7: 42).

1892 George and Weedon Grossmith, *The Diary of a Nobody*: 1 (4)

MAKE-UP: 'I will come tomorrow and bring my Irving make-up' (11: 116). 'Yes, it's a good make-up, isn't it? A regular-downright-respectable-funereal-first-class-City-firm-junior-clerk' (17: 170). [Also 11: 119 (twice).]

1894 Mark Twain, *Pudd'nhead* Wilson: 3

BACK-DOWN: Wilson was informed that his witnesses had been delayed, but would arrive presently; but he rose and said he should probably not have occasion to make use of their testimony. (An amused murmur ran through the room - 'It's a clean back-down! he gives up without hitting a lick!') (21: 212).

MARCH-PAST: The twins took a position near the door, the widow stood at Luigi's side, Rowena stood beside Angelo, and the march-past and the introductions began (6: 92).

ROUSTABOUT: 'It 'uz pow'ful hot, deckhan's en roustabouts 'uz sprawled aroun' asleep on de fo'cas'l'' (18: 184).

1895 Thomas Hardy, *Jude the Obscure*: 3

BREAKDOWN: Jude was in such physical pain from his unfortunate breakdown of the previous night (VI,7: 458).

SET-OFF: As a set-off against such discussions as these there had come an improvement in their pecuniary position (VI,3: 419).

TURN-OUT: An aged horse with a hanging head had been purchased for eight pounds at a sale, a creaking cart with a whity-brown tilt obtained for a few pounds more, and in this turn-out it became Jude's business thrice a week to carry loaves of bread to the villagers and solitary cotters immediately around Marygreen (I,5: 73).

1895 H G Wells, *The Time Machine*: 0

1897 H G Wells, *The Invisible Man*: 2 (3)

DRAWBACK: 'And I beheld, unclouded by doubt, a magnificent vision of all that Invisibility might mean to a man. The mystery, the power, the freedom. Drawbacks I saw none' (19: 140).

LOOK-OUT: [24: 180; 28: 211.]

1897 Henry James, *The Spoils of Poynton*: 3 (5)

DRAWBACK: [2: 11.]

KICK-UP: 'Then of course she won't like your changing.' 'I dare say she won't like it at all.' 'Do you mean to say you'll have a regular kick-up with her?' 'I don't exactly know what you mean by a regular kick-up' (8: 69).

SET-TO: 'But if you do have a set-to with her?' He paused so long for a reply that Fleda said: 'I don't think I know what you mean by a set-to.' 'Well, if she calls *you* names' (9: 70-71).

1897 Henry James, *What Maisie Knew*: 2

CASTAWAY: [9: 57.]

DRAWBACK: [20: 145.]

1898 Henry James, *The Turn of the Screw*: 1

BREAKDOWN: She could see what I myself saw: his derision, his amusement, his contempt for the breakdown of my resignation at being left alone and for the fine machinery I had set in motion to attract his attention to my slighted charms (12: 50).

1898 H G Wells, *The War of the Worlds*: 1 (2)

BREAKDOWN: There was very little excitement in the station, as the officials, failing to realize that anything further than a breakdown between Byfleet and Woking Junction had occurred, were running the theatre trains, which usually passed through Woking, round by Virginia Water. --- Few people, excepting the railway officials, connected the breakdown with the Martians (I,14: 130).

1900 Joseph Conrad, *Lord Jim*: 7 (13)

CASTAWAY: 'Those striving with unreasonable forces know it well, - the shipwrecked castaways in boats, wanderers lost in a desert' (7: 88). [Also 1: 6; 5: 48; 7: 81.]

LOOK-OUT: [10: 125; 14: 166; 44: 402.]

LOOK ROUND: 'Now you have been long enough here to have a good look round' (34: 325).

SET OUT: 'They caught me for that inquiry, you see,' he began, and for a while enlarged complainingly upon the inconveniences of daily attendance in court. --- 'What's the use of it? It is the stupidest set out you can imagine,' he pursued, hotly (6: 65). Only the other day an old fool he had never seen in his life came from some village miles away to find out if he should divorce his wife. --- Well, yes; a funny set out, upon the whole - the fool looked old enough to be his grandfather (27: 269).

STOWAWAY: My Jim, for the most part, skulked down below as though he had been a stowaway (19: 201).

SUCK IN: 'After a bit the old ship went down all on a sudden with a lurch to starboard - plop. The suck in was something awful. We never saw anything alive or dead come up' (13: 150).

TILT UP: He could depict to himself without hindrance the sudden swing upwards of the dark sky-line, the sudden tilt up of the vast plain of the sea (8: 96).

1901 H G Wells, *The First Men in the Moon*: 4 (5)

CASTAWAY: So we two poor terrestrial castaways, lost in that wild-growing moon jungle, crawled in terror before the sounds (11:

90). [Also 19: 167.]
DRAWBACK: [2: 33.]
FLY OFF: I was amazed to find how far I was from the moon. I had reckoned that not only should I have little or none of the 'kick-off' that the earth's atmosphere had given us at our start, but that the tangential 'fly off' of the moon's spin would be at least twenty-eight times less than the earth's (20: 180).
KICK-OFF: see FLY OFF, above.

1902 Joseph Conrad, *Heart of Darkness*: 5 (8)
CLEAN UP: 'My faith, your pilot-house wants a clean up!' (2: 76).
GET-UP: When near the buildings I met a white man, in such an unexpected elegance of get-up that in the first moment I took him for a sort of vision (1: 25).
LOOK-OUT: I had to keep a look-out for the signs of dead wood we could cut up (2: 49). It was the most hopeless look-out (2: 61). [Also 2: 62.]
SMASH-UP: I discovered that a lot of imported drainage-pipes for the settlement had been tumbled in there. There wasn't one that was not broken. It was a wanton smash-up (1: 24). I had no mind for a smash-up. You couldn't imagine a more deadly place for a shipwreck (2: 61).
TUCK IN: Why in the name of all the gnawing devils of hunger they didn't go for us - they were thirty to five - and have a good tuck in for once, amazes me now when I think of it (2: 59).

1902 Henry James, *The Wings of the Dove*: 7 (10)
BREAK-DOWN, BREAK-UP: 'There's a shadow across it.' 'That of what you allude to as some physical break-up?' 'Some physical break-down. Nothing less. She's scared. She has so much to lose' (20: 228).
LOOK-IN: They had left them for a look-in - the expression was

artfully Densher's - at St Mark (27: 319).

LOOK-OUT: She knew so much that her knowledge was what fairly kept her there, making her at times move endlessly between the small silk-covered sofa that stood for her in the firelight and the great grey map of Middlesex spread beneath her look-out (2: 22). That was one of the reflections made in our young woman's high retreat; she smiled from her lookout, in the silence that was only the fact of hearing irrelevant sounds (3: 41). But this imagination - the fancy of a possible link with the remarkable young thing from New York - *had* mustered courage: had perched, on the instant, at the clearest lookout it could find, and might be said to have remained there till, only a few months later, it had caught, in surprise and joy, the unmistakable flash of a signal (5: 71).

MAKE-UP: The way for her to meet criticism was evidently at the start to be sure her make-up was exact and that she looked at least no worse than usual (19: 217).

TURN ABOUT: It was for these things of interest, for Venice and the opportunity of Venice, for a prowl or two, as he called it, and a turn about, that he had looked his young man up (32: 391).

WIND-UP: Eugenio had the general tact of a residuary legatee - which was a character that could be definitely worn; whereas she could see Susie, in the event of her death, in no character at all. --- Eugenio had really done for her more than he probably knew - he didn't after all know everything - in having, for the wind-up of the autumn, on a weak word from her, so admirably, so perfectly established her (24: 283).

Many things, though not in many weeks, had come and gone since then, and one of the best of them, doubtless, had been the voyage itself, by the happy southern course, to the succession of Mediterranean ports, with the dazzled wind-up at Naples (5: 77).

1903 Henry James, *The Papers*: 2

TURN-OVER: If there had been no Papers there would have been no young friends for us of the figure we hint at, no chance mates, innocent and weary, yet acute even to penetration, who were apt to push off their plates and rest their elbows on the table in the interval between the turn-over of the pint-pot and the call for the awful glibness of their score (1: 136).
WIND-UP: [2: 153.]

1903 Henry James, *The Ambassadors*: 9

DRAWBACK: That would be the drawback of the bridling brightness. Yes, they would bridle and be bright; they would make the best of what was before them, but their observation would fail; it would be beyond them; they simply wouldn't understand (VIII,3: 234).
DROP BACK: 'And will he bring her back?' - Strether fell into the inquiry. But he wound it up as before. 'I don't know.' The way he wound it up, accompanied as this was with another drop back, another degustation of the Léoville, another wipe of his moustache and another good word for François, seemed to produce in his companion a slight irritation (III,I: 69).
GO-BY: The latter patted his shoulder while he thanked him, giving the go-by to the question of joining the Pococks (X,2: 307).
LOOK IN: Within three days, precisely, the situation on which he was to report had shown signs of an equilibrium; the effect of his look in at the hotel was to confirm this appearance (IX,2: 269).
LOOK-OUT: 'I'm always on the look-out for such chances for her' (VIII,4: 251).
LOOK ROUND: There were others who had invited him to a tryst at the inn and had even invoked his aid for a 'look round' at the beauties of Liverpool (I,1: 6).
RUNAWAY: What did the success of his proposal in fact resemble but the smash in which a regular runaway probably ends? (VII,1: 193).

TURN ABOUT: Strether took a turn about (IX,2: 273).

WIND-UP: Wouldn't *that* revelation practically amount to the wind-up of his career? (XII,3: 372).

1907 Joseph Conrad, *The Secret Agent*: 2

COUNT OUT: An inferior henchman of 'that brute Cheeseman' was up boring mercilessly a very thin House with some shamelessly cooked statistics. He, Toodles, hoped he would bore them into a count out every minute (10: 175).

GET-UP: His general get-up was that of a well-to-do mechanic in business for himself (2: 20).

1908 G K Chesterton, *The Man Who Was Thursday*: 2 (3)

GET-UP: 'That's a good get-up of yours,' said Syme, draining a glass of Mâcon; 'a lot better than old Gogol's. Even at the start I thought he was a bit too hairy' (8: 88).

MAKE-UP: 'I can't take my face off here,' replied Professor de Worms. 'It's rather an elaborate make-up' (8: 83). [Also 9: 99.]

1911 Joseph Conrad, *Under Western Eyes*: 1 (3)

LOOK-OUT: [III,1: 179; III,4: 225; III,4: 231.]

1911 D H Lawrence, *The White Peacock*: 4

GO-BETWEEN: Mayhew --- felt restrained and awkward in my presence. --- George was go-between. To me he was cautious and rather deferential, to Mayhew he was careless, and his attitude was tinged with contempt (III,5: 360).

LOOKOUT: 'She'll come round tomorrow - an' if she doesn't, it's her lookout' (III,1: 317).

PUT-OFF: 'Here, look at bun-bun! Have your nice rabbit! Hark at it squeaking!' The baby listened for a moment, then, deciding that this was only a put-off, began to cry again (III,4: 347).

SET-BACK: As I go to school by Old Brayford village in the morning the birds are thrilling wonderfully and everything seems stirring. Very likely there will be a set-back, and after that spring will come in truth (III,3: 338).

1913 D H Lawrence, *Sons and Lovers*: 5 (6)

GET-UP: 'My sirs!' exclaimed Mrs Radford, 'but you two's a pair of bright beauties, I must say! What's all that get-up for?' --- He in his dinner jacket, and Clara in her green dress and bare arms, were confused (12: 405).

LOOKOUT: 'It's a poor lookout' (6: 164). 'That's *your* lookout!' (12: 405).

MAKE-UP: 'I can only give friendship - it's all I'm capable of - it's a flaw in my make-up' (9: 271).

SET-BACK: 'Look at her mouth - made for passion - and the very set-back of her throat - -' He threw his head back in Clara's defiant manner (8: 231).

TAKE-OFF: He sat at the head of the table, his mobile face, with eyes that could be so beautiful, shining with tenderness or dancing with laughter, now taking on one expression and then another, in imitation of various people he was mocking. --- The whole family loved a 'take-off' more than anything (9: 266).

1915 D H Lawrence, *The Rainbow*: 3 (4)

GO-BY: 'You can't wear water out. No, my boy; it'll give you the go-by' (9: 245).

LOOK-OUT: It was dedicated: 'To my wife, Millicent Maud Pearse, in whom I embrace the generous spirit of England.' 'If he embraces no more than the spirit of England,' said Tom Brangwen, 'it's a bad look-out for him' (7: 197). 'It was a lot of use putting those ten loads of cinders on th' road. They'll be washed to kingdom-come if it doesn't alter. Well, it's our Fred's look-out, if they are. He's top-sawyer as far as those things go' (9: 245).

STAND-BACK: This was a great stand-back to Ursula, who suffered agonies when she thought a person disliked her (12: 335).

1915 Charlotte Perkins Gilman, *Herland*: 0

1915 Ford Madox Ford, *The Good Soldier*: 2
> **BREAKDOWN**: Upon her return from Nauheim Leonora had completely broken down - because she knew she could trust Edward. That seems odd but, if you know anything about breakdowns, you will know that by the ingenious torments that fate prepares for us, these things come as soon as, a strain having relaxed, there is nothing more to be done (IV,2: 183).
> **BURST OUT**: I was quite astonished, during his final burst out to me --- to observe how literary and how just his expressions were. --- Anyhow, it burst out of him on that horrible night (I,3: 32).

1918 Lytton Strachey, *Eminent Victorians*: 2
> **BREAKDOWN**: What had occurred was, in brief, the complete breakdown of our medical arrangements at the seat of war ('Florence Nightingale', 2: 136).
> **GO-BETWEEN**: It is significant that the go-between who acted as the Government's agent in its negotiations with Gordon was an imperialist - Lord Wolseley ('The End of General Gordon': 268).

1920 Sinclair Lewis, *Main Street*: 11
> **GET-UP**: 'Uh - Will, I wonder if that young man in white flannel trousers, at church this morning, was this Valborg person that they're all talking about?' 'Yump. That's him. Wasn't that the darndest get-up he had on!' (XXVIII,3: 308).
> **GIT-UP-AND-GIT**: 'Maybe he is kind of a roughneck, but you got to hand it to him; he's got more git-up-and-git than any fellow that ever hit this burg' (XXXV,3: 381).
> **HOLD-UP**: 'But I don't care much for these plays. What I like is a good movie, with auto accidents and hold-ups, and some git to it, and not all this talky-talk' (XVIII,6: 212).
> **KNOCK-OUT**: It was the sort of farce which is advertised in 'school entertainment' catalogues as: Riproaring knock-out. 5 m., 3 f., time 2 hrs., interior set, popular with churches and all high-class occasions

(XVIII,1: 204).

LEAN-TO: From the front, Howland & Gould's grocery was smug enough, but attached to the rear was a lean-to of storm-streaked pine lumber with a sanded tar roof (XXIX,4: 324).

LOOK-IN: 'I've got to hand it to you. You're consistent all right. I'd of thought that after getting this look-in at a lot of good decent farmers, you'd get over this high-art stuff, but you hang right on' (XVI,3: 187).

MIX-UP: 'Today. Oh, there wasn't much of anything: couple chumps with bellyaches, and a sprained wrist, and a fool woman that thinks she wants to kill herself because her husband doesn't like her and - Just routine work.' 'But the unhappy woman doesn't sound routine!' 'Her? Just a case of nerves. You can't do much with these marriage mix-ups' (VIII,1: 91).

SET-TO: 'This foreman and I have some great set-to's. He's a regular old-line party-member. Too dogmatic' (X,3: 112).

SHOW-DOWN: 'You do like to talk, but at a show-down you'd prefer Sam Clark to any damn long-haired artist' (XVI,3: 187).

TRYOUT: He was thrilled --- by a New York theatrical manager down for the tryout of a play (XXXVIII,5: 404).

TURNOVER: 'And you listen when Harry Haydock tries to show off and talk about turnovers and credits and things you know lots better than he does' (XXI,3: 240).

Period 2: 1814-1920. A general survey

Whereas, in the period 1726-1813, half the works sampled were found to contain no NPV, and no work contained more than 2, the situation is very different in the period 1814-1920.

Among the 58 works sampled there are only 4 works - all of them short (novella-length) - in which I have found no NPV:

1878 Henry James, *Daisy Miller*: 0
1888 Henry James, *The Aspern Papers*: 0
1895 H G Wells, *The Time Machine*: 0
1915 Charlotte Perkins Gilman, *Herland*: 0

The remaining 54 works all contain one or more NPVs. Of these, the following 28 works contain 4 or more NPVs.

1920 Sinclair Lewis, *Main Street*: 11
1903 Henry James, *The Ambassadors*: 9
1868 Wilkie Collins, *The Moonstone*: 8 (16)
1889 Mark Twain, *A Connecticut Yankee at King Arthur's Court*: 8 (11)
1847-48 William Thackeray, *Vanity Fair*: 7 (17)
1860-61 Charles Dickens, *Great Expectations*: 7 (13)
1900 Joseph Conrad, *Lord Jim*: 7 (13)
1902 Henry James, *The Wings of the Dove*: 7 (10)
1855-57 Charles Dickens, *Little Dorrit*: 7 (9)
1836-37 Charles Dickens, *The Pickwick Papers*: 7 (8)
1854-55 Elizabeth Gaskell, *North and South*: 6 (20)
1816 Jane Austen, *Emma*: 6 (11)
1890 Rudyard Kipling, *Plain Tales from the Hills*: 6 (8)
1890 William Morris, *News from Nowhere*: 6 (8)
1858 Anthony Trollope, *Doctor Thorne*: 5 (10)
1857 Anthony Trollope, *Barchester Towers*: 5 (8)
1902 Joseph Conrad, *Heart of Darkness*: 5 (8)
1913 D H Lawrence, *Sons and Lovers*: 5 (6)
1814 Jane Austen, *Mansfield Park* 4 (12)
1845 Benjamin Disraeli, *Sybil*: 4 (8)
1881 Henry James, *The Portrait of a Lady*: 4 (8)
1866 George Eliot, *Felix Holt, the Radical*: 4 (7)
1871-72: George Eliot, *Middlemarch*: 4 (5)

1901 H G Wells, *The First Men in the Moon*: 4 (5)
1877 Henry James, *The American*: 4
1888 Edward Bellamy, *Looking Backward, 2000-1887*: 4
1891 Thomas Hardy, *Tess of the d'Urbervilles*: 4
1911 D H Lawrence, *The White Peacock*: 4

In the 58 works sampled from the period 1814-1920 I found 75 different NPVs in 337 occurrences (averaging 4.5 occurrences per NPV and 5.8 occurrences per work). A frequency count shows great differences. The following are the 4 most frequently occurring NPVs in the material:

LOOK-OUT:	73 occurrences	=	22%
DRAWBACK:	61 -	=	18%
TURN-OUT:	22 -	=	7%
CASTAWAY:	18 -	=	5%

Together these 4 words account for 174 of the 337 occurrences (= 52%). The remaining NPVs occur so sparsely in the material (from 12 to 1 occurrences, or from 3.6% to 0.3%) that differences in their relative frequency is of doubtful significance.

If, instead of examining how many times each NPV occurs, we ask how many different writers it is used by, we find that the following 10 NPVs are used by 5 or more of the 24 writers we have examined:

LOOK-OUT:	15 writers	
DRAWBACK:	11	-
BREAKDOWN:	10	-
CASTAWAY:	10	-
MAKE-UP:	7	-
GET-UP:	6	-

GO-BETWEEN:	6	-
SET-OFF:	6	-
TURN-OUT:	6	-
BREAK-UP:	5	-

The significance of NPVs in periods 1 and 2
Our figures suggest an increasing acceptance of NPVs through the two periods we have examined. The fact that the highest number of NPVs is found in the most recent of the novels - a work published after World War I - is, of course, hardly accidental. Nor does it look like an accident that the four novels with the highest 'score' (8-11 per work) are all from the second half of the second period, and that three of their authors are American (though such very different Americans as Sinclair Lewis, Henry James, and Mark Twain). But there is no obvious watershed anywhere in period 2: the figure 6 is reached as early as 1816 (by Jane Austen's *Emma*), and the figure 7 as early as 1836-37 (by Dickens's *Pickwick Papers*).

What may be the reason for the increasing popularity of NPVs? The answer to this question should perhaps be sought in the periods here examined. For in those two periods the NPVs are still, so to speak, on probation, still feeling their way; after 1920 follows the deluge.

A study of the meanings and implications of the NPVs here recorded brings to light at least two important peculiarities:

(1) NPVs tend to have restricted or specialised (not to say exclusive) meanings. Many of them belong to expert jargons and are felt as the *mots propres* in special contexts. In the word-list which follows below, a number of NPVs are expressly characterised as jargon words; but the reader may well arrive at the conclusion that many, perhaps most, of the words in the list seem the proper pseudo- or semi-technical words in well-defined

situations. As examples of NPVs which border on jargon may be mentioned: *break-up, get-up, hold-up, lean-to, runaway, shake-down, stand-by.*

(2) On account of their relative freshness and unignorable components NPVs are forceful, even aggressive and sometimes almost vulgar, when it comes to calling up a mental image or evoking associations. Words like *blow-out, break-down, get-up, go-between, look-out, mix-up, put-off, smash-up* are patently more illustrative and emphatic than near-synonyms like *feast, collapse, costume, intermediary, observation post, confusion, evasion, destruction.*

In this there is, of course, no suggestion that NPVs are stylistically 'better' than their more Latinate counterparts. They do, no doubt, possess force and transparency, but they may occasionally seem lacking in taste and finesse. They have an up-to-date ring but may be found wanting in tradition. They often tempt writers into wordplay, sometimes subtle (as frequently in Henry James), sometimes heavyhanded.

It would seem a pretty safe guess, demanding no great psychological penetration, that the use of NPVs gives both writer and reader an agreeable feeling of being particular in an unpedantic way, with it, even (in a sense) 'heroic', and that this is one of the main reasons for their eventual triumph - a victory which has, paradoxically, robbed them of some of their native panache. It should be noted that in the quotations the NPVs occur with especial frequency in reported speech and in passages that are meant to sound informal or colloquial. It seems clear that the literary artist has taken to the NPVs largely for their unliterary get-up.

The following word-list embraces all NPV occurrences quoted in the above chronological surveys of periods 1 and 2; only real quotations are included, not mere references (in square brackets).

Each headword is followed by:

(1) (Between quotation marks): an attempt to suggest the pictorial or associational force of the word.

(2) In some cases, a bracketed indication of the type of jargon which the world implies.

(3) A semantic (ie dictionary-type) definition.

(4) A list of the word's occurrences in the quotations of the chronological surveys. Each quoted work is identified by the year of its publication, the author's last name, and one distinctive word from the title. If the survey quotes several occurrences of the same NPV in the same work, they are distinguished by figures (1, 2, 3, etc) after the title.

List of NPVs in quotations from periods 1 and 2

BACK-DOWN: 'retreating from high point', admission that one is wrong, withdrawal of claims, climb-down: 1894 Twain *Pudd'nhead*

BLOW-OUT: 'puffing up, eg of stomach', feast, tuck-in = 1845 Disraeli Sybil 1-2, 1889 Twain *Yankee*

BLOW-UP: 'puffing up something till it bursts', disturbance: 1847 Brontë *Jane*

BREAK-DOWN: 'falling down, becoming unfit for use', collapse, failure

(1) of a concrete structure, eg a carriage: 1836-37 Dickens *Pickwick*

(2) of an abstract structure, eg a system or arrangement: 1888 Bellamy *Looking*, 1890 Morris *News*, 1898 Wells *War*, 1918 Strachey *Victorians*

(3) of somebody's physical, mental, or moral health: 1868 Collins *Moonstone*, 1895 Hardy *Jude*, 1898 James *Screw*, 1902 James

Wings, 1915 Ford *Soldier*

BREAK-UP: 'splitting into several pieces', disintegration of a Whole, eg

    (1) a party: 1814 Austen *Mansfield*, 1857 Trollope *Barchester*

    (2) a household or family: 1818 Austen *Persuasion*, 1860 Collins *Woman*, 1881 James *Portrait*

    (3) a town or society: 1890 Morris *News* 1-2

    (4) somebody's endurance: 1902 James *Wings*

BURST OUT: 'something that forces its way into the open', violent outburst: 1915 Ford *Soldier*

CASTAWAY: 'somebody thrown away or rejected', somebody thrown ashore or (metaphorically) left to his/her fate, eg

    (1) a shipwrecked person: 1854-55 Gaskell *North*, 1900 Conrad *Jim*, 1901 Wells *Moon*

    (2) a religious outsider: 1847 Brontë *Jane*, 1847-48 Thackeray *Vanity* 1, 1857 Trollope *Barchester*

    (3) a social outsider: 1847-48 Thackeray *Vanity* 2, 1855-57 Dickens *Dorrit*, 1858 Trollope *Thorne*, 1891 Hardy *Tess*

CLEAN-UP: 'cleaning all the way', thorough cleaning: 1902 Conrad *Heart*

COME-DOWN: 'sinking to a lower, humbler level', reduction to a lower social position, loss of prestige: 1877 James *American*

COUNT OUT: 'making a complete count, or counting somebody out of the game' (parliamentary jargon) the Speaker's bringing the sitting to a close when too few members are present: 1907 Conrad *Secret*

CRY-OUT: 'cry that forces its way out', exclamation of surprise, outcry: 1816 Austen *Emma*

CUT-AWAY: 'a whole from which something has been cut away' (tailors' jargon) tailcoat: 1855-57 Dickens *Dorrit*

DRAWBACK: 'something that retracts from something, or reduces its value':

(1) reduction: 1811 Austen *Sense*

(2) inconvenience: 1759-67 Sterne *Tristram*, 1814 Austen *Mansfield* 1-2-3, 1816 Austen *Emma*, 1836-37 Dickens *Pickwick* 1-2, 1847-48 Thackeray *Vanity*, 1849 Brontë *Shirley*, 1849-50 Dickens *David*, 1854-55 Gaskell *North*, 1855-57 Dickens *Dorrit*, 1857 Trollope *Barchester* 1-2, 1858 Trollope *Thorne*, 1860 Collins *Woman*, 1860-61 Dickens *Expectations*, 1868 Collins *Moonstone*, 1881 James *Portrait*, 1886 James *Bostonians*, 1890 Morris *News*, 1890 Kipling *Plain*, 1897 Wells *Invisible*, 1903 James *Ambassadors*.

DROP BACK: 'reverting to a former position', return to an earlier physical or mental attitude: 1903 James *Ambassadors*.

FALL-OFF: 'dropping from a high level' (commercial jargon) lower standard: 1877 James *American*

FLY-OFF: 'flying away from a given course' (intended astronautical jargon) leaving orbit along tangent, cf KICK-OFF: 1901 Wells *Moon*

GADABOUT: 'somebody who moves about like a gadfly', a person who travels much: 1877 James *American*

GET-UP: 'bringing about a visible effect', costume which is

(1) suitable for a special purpose: 1858 Trollope *Thorne*, 1907 Conrad *Secret*, 1908 Chesterton *Thursday*

(2) (exaggeratedly) elegant: 1902 Conrad *Heart*, 1913 Lawrence *Sons*

(3) odd rather than elegant: 1866 Eliot *Felix*, 1920 Lewis *Main*

GIT-UP-AND-GIT = get-up-and-get: 'rising and getting results', energy, initiative, push: 1920 Lewis *Main*

GIVE-AWAY: 'as if it were a present' (commercial jargon) low price: 1889 Twain *Yankee*

GO-BETWEEN: 'somebody who moves between two persons or groups', messenger, agent, intermediary: 1851-53 Gaskell *Cranford*, 1855-57 Dickens *Dorrit*, 1858 Trollope *Thorne*, 1868 Collins *Moonstone*, 1911 Lawrence *Peacock*, 1918 Strachey *Victorians*

GO-BY: 'passing by without stopping' - *give the go-by*: ignore, pretend not to notice: 1847-48 Thackeray *Vanity*, 1903 James *Ambassadors*, 1915 Lawrence *Rainbow*

GO-OFF: 'leaving a place', start, time: 1866 Eliot *Felix*

HOLD-UP: 'holding up one's hands', robbery: 1920 Lewis *Main*

KICK-OFF: 'giving a violent push' (intended astronautical jargon) impetus given to moonship by earth's atmosphere, cf FLY-OFF: 1901 Wells *Moon*

KICK-UP: 'violent, aggressive movement':

(1) (literal) kick with hind-legs: 1860 Dickens *Expectations*.

(2) violent dancing: 1891 Hardy *Tess*

(3) a quarrel, a set-to: 1897 James *Poynton*

KNOCK-DOWN: 'hitting somebody so that he falls' (boxing jargon):

(1) a fall in a boxing match: 1888 Bellamy *Looking*

(2) (figuratively) an overwhelming mass or power: 1836-37 Dickens *Pickwick*

KNOCK-OUT: 'something overwhelming, irresistible', a farce to make you burst with laughter: 1920 Lewis *Main*

LAY-OUT: 'arranging parts so as to form a pattern or whole' (stage and circus jargon) a composition of parts which form a whole, a set-out: 1889 Twain *Yankee* 1-2-3

LEAN-TO: 'something leaning against something' (technical jargon or pejorative) a building with a sloping roof resting on the side of another building: 1890 Morris *News*, 1920 Lewis *Main*

LOCK-OUT: 'preventing somebody from getting in', employers' refusal to let employees go to work: 1888 Bellamy *Looking*, 1890 Morris *News*

LOCK-UP: 'preventing somebody from getting out', prison: 1860-61 Dickens *Expectations*

LOOK AROUND: 'looking in all directions', examination of what is around one: 1851-53 Gaskell *Cranford*

LOOK-IN: 'observing something that is usually closed to the outside', brief visit to a house or (humorously) a tourist attraction: 1902 James *Wings*, 1903 James *Ambassadors*, 1920 Lewis *Main*

LOOK-OUT: 'observing an open or wide space from a closed or narrow space':

(1) (nautical jargon) a look-out man: 1849-50 Dickens *David* 2

(2) observation post: 1889 Twain *Yankee* 2, 1902 James *Wings* 2-3 - *(be, be placed, be situated, be stationed) on the look-out (for)*: 1749 Fielding *Tom*, 1816 Austen *Emma* 2, 1847-48 Thackeray *Vanity* 1, 1854 Dickens *Hard* 1, 1854-55 Gaskell *North* 2, 1855 Trollope *Warden*, 1860 Collins *Woman*, 1866 Eliot *Felix*, 1868 Collins *Moonstone*, 1871-72 Eliot *Middlemarch*, 1881 James *Portrait*, 1890 Morris *News*, 1890 Kipling *Plain*, 1903 James *Ambassadors*

(3) act of keeping watch: 1816 Austen *Emma* 1, 1860-61 Dickens *Expectations* - *keep a (sharp) look-out (for)*: Austen 1814 *Mansfield*, 1836-37 Dickens *Pickwick*, 1847 Brontë *Jane*, 1854 Dickens *Hard* 3, 1889 Twain *Yankee* 1, 1902 Conrad *Heart* 1 - *keep a double look-out on*: 1849-50 Dickens *David*

(4) view, prospect: 1854-55 Gaskell *North* 1, 1855-57 Dickens *Dorrit* 2, 1860-61 Dickens *Expectations* 1

(5) outlook, prospects, hope: - *a bad/blank/hopeless/poor look-out*: 1886 James *Bostonians*, 1902 Conrad *Heart* 2, 1913 Lawrence *Sons* 1, 1915 Lawrence *Rainbow* 1

(6) view, eyes: 1902 James *Wings* 1

(7) view, way of looking at things: 1854 Dickens *Hard* 2

(8) concern, business: - *it's your/his (etc) look-out*: it is your affair, responsibility: 1847-48 Thackeray *Vanity* 2, 1854 Dickens *Hard* 4, 1855-57 Dickens *Dorrit* 1, 1857 Trollope *Barchester*, 1858 Trollope *Thorne*, 1911 Lawrence *Peacock*, 1913 Lawrence *Sons* 2,

1915 Lawrence *Rainbow*

LOOK ROUND: 'looking in all directions', (understatement for) inspection, search: 1891 Hardy *Tess*, 1900 Conrad *Jim*, 1903 James *Ambassadors*

LOOK UP: 'directing one's eyes upwards', an upward glance: 1759-67 Sterne *Tristram*, 1868 Collins *Moonstone*

MAKE-UP: 'putting something together, composition':

(1) (stage or circus jargon) powder, paint, etc. put on the face by actor or circus clown, or by somebody assuming a false identity, or by a woman: 1866 Eliot *Felix*, 1889 Twain *Yankee*, 1890 Kipling *Plain* 2, 1892 Grossmith *Diary* 1-2, 1902 James *Wings*, 1908 Chesterton *Thursday*

(2) a trick: 1890 Kipling *Plain* 1

(3) a combination of qualities, a character: 1913 Lawrence *Sons*

MARCH-PAST: 'passing somebody with measured steps' (military jargon) parading past an officer who takes the salute, or (metaphorically and humorously) entering a room in single file: 1890 Kipling *Plain*, 1894 Twain *Pudd'nhead*

MIX-UP: 'putting things in disorder', confusion, muddle: 1920 Lewis *Main*

PASSOVER: 'passing by without noticing or touching', Jewish feast (reference to *Exod* xii.23): 1847 Disraeli *Tancred* 1-2

PULL-UP: 'pulling the reins' (technical jargon for stopping a horse) a sudden stop or check - *a sudden/strong pull-up*: 1836-37 Dickens *Pickwick*, 1854-55 Gaskell *North*, 1871-72 Eliot *Middlemarch*

PUSH AWAY (literal): 1854-55 Gaskell *North*

PUT-OFF: 'removing something that should be near':

(1) postponement: 1816 Austen *Emma*

(2) excuse for not doing something, evasion: 1911 Lawrence *Peacock*

ROUND-UP: 'going from place to place, making a complete circle' (journalistic jargon) visits to neighbours, friends, colleagues: 1889 Twain *Yankee*

ROUSTABOUT: '(perhaps) somebody who drifts around, or is driven from place to place', deck hand or wharf labourer: 1894 Twain *Pudd'nhead*

RUNAWAY: 'somebody escaping from authority':
    (1) escaped convict: 1860-61 Dickens *Expectations*
    (2) (metaphorically) two people escaping from the stable pattern of their lives, or a situation which runs away with them: 1903 James *Ambassadors*
    (3) (jocularly) somebody who has temporarily left her companions: 1778 Burney *Evelina*

SEND-OFF: 'taking leave of somebody' (sports reporters' jargon) wishing somebody a good fight: 1889 Twain *Yankee*

SET-BACK: 'holding, forcing something backwards':
    (1) return to earlier weather conditions: 1911 Lawrence *Peacock*
    (2) the way something is held further back than usual: 1913 Lawrence *Sons*

SET-DOWN: 'placing somebody in a lower position', a statement which humiliates the listener, a put-down: 1813 Austen *Pride*, 1868 Collins *Moonstone*

SET-OFF: 'placing something opposite something else' (commercial jargon) something of the same financial, moral, or spiritual value as something else: 1847-48 Thackeray *Vanity*, 1849-50 Dickens *David*, 1855-57 Dickens *Dorrit*, 1871-72 Eliot *Middlemarch*, 1881 James *Portrait*, 1888 Bellamy *Looking*, 1895 Hardy *Jude*

SET-OUT: 'spreading something', a composition of parts which form an obvious or mysterious pattern:
    (1) spread of food: 1816 Austen *Emma*
    (2) lay-out of an artistic whole: 1836-37 Dickens *Pickwick*
    (3) peculiar group of people: 1854 Dickens *Hard*

(4) peculiar scene or situation: 1900 Conrad *Jim* 1-2

SET-TO: 'starting something suddenly', a round, etc:
    (1) of rat-hunting: 1818 Austen *Persuasion*
    (2) of quarrelling: 1897 James *Poynton*, 1920 Lewis *Main*

SHAKE-DOWN: 'scattering, arranging something on the floor', a primitive straw bed or (disparagingly) any bed: 1854 Dickens *Hard*, 1860-61 Dickens *Expectations*, 1889 Twain *Yankee*

SHAKE-UP: 'turning somebody's world or ideas upside down', bad shock: 1868 Collins *Moonstone*

SHOW-DOWN: 'putting the cards on the table' - *at a showdown*: in an emergency: 1920 Lewis *Main*

SMASH-UP: 'breaking things violently', wanton destruction, or destruction by accident: 1902 Conrad *Heart* 1-2

STAND-BACK: 'stepping backwards in defeat', humiliation, set-back: 1915 Lawrence *Rainbow*

STAND-BY: 'supporter who is always near', something to be relied on, eg a subject for conversation: 1886 James *Bostonians*

START-UP: 'something that springs up unexpectedly', a sudden event: 1845 Disraeli *Sybil*

STICK-OUT: 'offering continued resistance or opposition', strike: 1845 Disraeli *Sybil* 1-2

STOW-AWAY: 'somebody hiding among the cargo', a person hiding on a ship to get a free passage: 1900 Conrad *Jim*

SUCK IN: 'drawing in air by the mouth', the sucking power that pulls people and things downwards under the water: 1900 Conrad *Jim*

TAKE-IN: 'drawing or luring somebody into a trap', deceit: 1778 Burney *Evelina*, 1814 Austen *Mansfield*, 1857 Trollope *Barchester*

TAKE-OFF: 'pulling the mask or face off somebody else and putting it on', copy, imitation: 1913 Lawrence *Sons*

THROW-BACK: 'holding, pulling, forcing something backwards':
    (1) the way something is held further back than usual, set-back:

1851-53 Gaskell *Cranford*

(2) a characteristic representing an earlier evolutionary stage: 1890 Kipling *Plain*

TILT-UP: 'occupying an upward sloping position', eg the apparent slope of the sea: 1900 Conrad *Jim*

TOSS-UP: 'throwing a coin into the air', a matter of chance, something unpredictable: 1860-61 Dickens *Expectations* 1-2, 1871-72 Eliot *Middlemarch*

TRY-OUT: 'testing something in practice before accepting it' (theatrical jargon) first performances of a play outside the metropolis: 1920 Lewis *Main*

TUCK-IN: 'pushing something into a narrow space', a hearty meal: 1886 Hardy *Mayor*, 1902 Conrad *Heart*

TUCK-OUT: 'pushing something into a narrow space to make it swell'(school jargon) a feast (esp consisting of sweets), a blow-out, a tuck-in: 1847-48 Thackeray *Vanity*

TURN ABOUT: 'moving in various directions', a stroll: 1902 James *Wings*, 1903 James *Ambassadors*

TURN-OUT: 'changing direction/position/shape and coming out into the open':

(1) a driving equipage: 1836-37 Dickens *Pickwick*, 1847-48 Thackeray *Vanity* 2, 1855-57 Dickens *Dorrit* 1-2, 1891 Hardy *Tess*, 1895 Hardy *Jude* (ironical use)

(2) the style in which people, coaches, horses, etc. are got up: 1847-48 Thackeray *Vanity* 1, 1890 Kipling *Plain*

(3) a strike: 1845 Disraeli *Sybil* 1-2, 1854-55 Gaskell *North* 3

(4) a striker: 1854-55 Gaskell *North* 1-2

(5) a signal to rise: 1847-48 Thackeray *Vanity* 3

TURN-OVER: 'something moving from one side or state to another' (commercial jargon):

(1) goods produced and sold, stock acquired and realised, money made and spent: 1920 Lewis *Main*

(2) (metaphorically and humorously) glasses emptied and refilled: 1903 James *Papers*

WIND-UP: 'rolling something into a ball', conclusion (esp one which gives a final shape to some story or sequence of events): 1816 Austen *Emma*, 1877 James *American*, 1886 Hardy *Mayor*, 1902 James *Wings* 1-2, 1903 James *Ambassadors*.

Postscript: After 1920

After 1920 came the deluge. Space forbids me to do more than cite a few striking examples.

The first novel in my material to beat Sinclair Lewis's 1920 record of 11 was (it can hardly come as a surprise; I list the NPVs without quotations and references): 1922 James Joyce: *Ulysses*: 18 (19): *blowout, botchup, breakdown, brushup, comedown, fallback, goby, go-off* (twice), *lookin, mouseabout, putoff, sendoff, setdown, shakedown, stowaway, throwaway, toss up, turnover.*

I have found only 2 inter-war novelists to compete with Joyce, both of them American crime-writers:

1929 Dashiell Hammet: *Red Harvest*: 20 (31),
  breakdown, come-back, crush-out (2), *cut-up, frame-up* (2), *get-away* (7), *get-together, hideout, knockout, knock-over, lay-out, look around, set-up, shake-down, showdown, stack-up, stick-up* (3), *tip-off* (2), *walk-out, wash-out.*

1939 Raymond Chandler: *The Big Sleep*: 17 (24):
  build-up, bump-off, come-on, cover-up (2), *get-away, get-up, hangover* (2), *hideaway, hideout, hold-up, layout* (5), *line-up,*

pushover (2), *set-up, stand-off, stick-up, write-up.*

After World War II the use of NPVs in fiction seems to have been steadily increasing. The all-time record in my material is held by: 1977 John Le Carré: *The Honourable Schoolboy*: 48 (74):

answer-back, blow-out, breakdown (2), *breakthrough, break-up, check-in, cutout, drag-up, fallback* (4), *follow-through, follow-up* (2), *fuck-up* (3), *get-together, handout* (2), *handover, hangover, kickback, kiss-off* (2), *layabout, layout* (2), *lead-in, look round, make-up* (4), *march-past, pay-off, pickup, pin-up, press-up, printout, pullout* (4), *pullover* (2), *put-up, rollback, rundown* (2), *run-in, snarl-up, standby* (3), *stopover* (2), *take-off* (2), *takeover* (4), *throwaway, tie-up, tip-off, toss-up, turn-round, turn-up* (2), *washout, wrap-up.*

Close runners-up are:

1976 Lisa Alther: *Kinflicks*: 39 (69);
1977 John Fowles: *Daniel Martin*: 38 (62);
1980 William Styron: *Sophie's Choice* 31 (64).

Other novelists use NPVs with somewhat greater moderation. But I have only found one novel after 1920 which contains no NPVs at all (as always: barring oversights). It may be as little of a surprise as James Joyce's above-mentioned short-lived record:

1927 Virginia Woolf: *To the Lighthouse*: 0

NOTES

Two helpful special dictionaries are A P Cowie & R Mackin, *Oxford Dictionary of Current Idiomatic English Volume 1: Verbs with Prepositions and Particles*, London, Oxford University Press (first publ. 1975), and Rosemary Courtney, *Longman Dictionary of Phrasal Verbs*, Longman Group Limited (first publ. 1983).

The most helpful recent study (with references to earlier studies) is Knud Sørensen, 'Phrasal Verb into Noun', *Neuphilologische Mitteilungen* 87/2 (1986), 272-283 = *English Past and Present. A Selection of Essays by Knud Sørensen presented to him on his sixtieth birthday*, ed. by Marianne Powell and Bent Preisler, *Acta Jutlandica* LXIV:1, Humanities Series 62, 148-159, Aarhus University Press, 1988.

An important statistical treatment of NPVs is U. Lindelöf, 'English Verb-Adverb Groups Converted into Nouns', *Societas Scientiarum Fennica: Commentationes Humanarum Litterarum*, IX,5, Helsingfors 1938.

Lindelöf attempts to determine the total number of NPVs extant in the English language in different periods. Thus, he has found 4 NPVs recorded before 1500 (*run-about, lean-to, stand-fra, sit-up*), 24 new ones in the 16th century, 27 additional ones in the 17th century, 33 more in the 18th century - after which the number increases considerably. Lindelöf's sources are chiefly *The New English Dictionary + Supplement* and some American slang dictionaries.

Thus, Lindelöf aims at finding the absolute number of NPVs in various periods, while my aim is to discover what and how many NPVs were current in English literary prose in various periods (esp 1726-1813 and 1814-1920). In both cases, what is found can be no more than an approximation to the truth.

List of editions quoted

The following editions are quoted in the chronological surveys above. Abbreviations: NCE = Norton Critical Edition, OUP = Oxford University Press, PEL = Penguin English Library, PMC = Penguin Modern Classics.

Jane Austen, *Emma*, PEL 1974
- *Mansfield Park*, PEL 1972
- *Persuasion*, PEL 1974
- *Pride and Prejudice*, PEL 1974
- *Sense and Sensibility*, PEL 1974

Edward Bellamy, *Looking Backward*, Penguin Classics 1987
Charlotte Brontë, *Jane Eyre*, PEL 1972
- *Shirley*, PEL 1975

Francis Burney, *Evelina*, OUP paperback 1970
C K Chesterton, *The Man Who Was Thursday*, Penguin Books 1938
Wilkie Collins, *The Moonstone*, The Nelson Classics, n.d.
- *The Woman in White*, PEL 1977

Joseph Conrad, *Heart of Darkness*, PMC 1976
- *Lord Jim*, M Dent & Sons Ltd, London 1940
- *The Secret Agent*, PMC 1973
- *Under Western Eyes*, PMC 1973

Charles Dickens, *David Copperfield*, Collins, London n.d.
- *Great Expectations*, PEL 1973
- *Hard Times*, PEL 1969
- *Little Dorrit*, PEL 1967
- *The Pickwick Papers*, PEL 1972

Benjamin Disraeli, *Sybil*, PEL 1980
- *Tancred*, John Lane, The Bodley Head 1927

George Eliot, *Felix Holt*, PEL 1972
- *Middlemarch*, PEL 1965

53

Henry Fielding, *Tom Jones*, NCE 1973
Ford Madox Ford, *The Good Soldier*, PMC 1977
Elizabeth Gaskell, *Cranford, Cousin Phillis*, PEL 1976
- *North and South*, PEL 1976
George & Weedon Grossmith, *The Diary of a Nobody*, PMC 1977
Thomas Hardy, *Jude the Obscure*, PEL 1979
- *The Mayor of Casterbridge*, Macmillan, London 1973
- *Tess of the d'Urbervilles*, NCE 1965
Henry James, *The Ambasadors*, PMC 1976
- *The American*, Macmillan, London, 1921
- *The Aspern Papers and Other Stories* (incl. 'The Papers'), PMC 1976
- *The Bostonians*, PMC 1982
- *The Portrait of a Lady*, NCE 1975
- *The Spoils of Poynton*, PMC 1972
- *The Turn of the Screw*, NCE 1966
- *What Maisie Knew*, PMC 1981
- *The Wings of the Dove*, PMC 1976
Rudyard Kipling, *Plain Tales from the Hills*, Penguin Classics 1987
D H Lawrence, *The Rainbow*, Penguin Books 1973
- *Sons and Lovers*, Penguin Books 1972
- *The White Peacock*, PEL 1984
Sinclair Lewis, *Main Street*, PMC 1985
William Morris, *News from Nowhere*, Routledge and Kegan Paul, London 1970
Laurence Sterne, *Tristram Shandy*, NCE 1980
Lytton Strachey, *Eminent Victorians*, Penguin Books 1948
William Thackeray, *Vanity Fair*, PEL 1971
Anthony Trollope, *Barchester Towers*, PEL 1983
- *Doctor Thorne*, The World's Classics, OUP 1980
- *The Warden*, The World's Classics, OUP 1980

Mark Twain, *A Connecticut Yankee at King Arthur's Court*, PEL 1979
- *Pudd'nhead Wilson*, PEL 1975

H G Wells, *The First Men in the Moon*, Collins, London & Glasgow n.d.
- *The Invisible Man*, Collins, London & Glasgow 1971
- *Three Novels* (incl. *The War of the Worlds*), Heineman, London 1972.

Henrik Gottlieb

IDIOMS INTO DANISH
Principles and Design of a Bilingual Dictionary of Current Idiomatic English Usage: The English-Danish Idiomatic Dictionary

THE IDIOM CONCEPT
In English, the word 'idiom' covers a wide range of meanings, including (1) 'specific mode of expression', (2) 'native tongue' and (3) 'multi-word unit with non-transparent meaning'. [1] The common denominator here is the notion of "inside knowledge", and although I shall focus on the third sense of 'idiom', it is interesting to see that senses one and two give clues to the special nature of idioms in the 'semantically opaque multi-word unit'-sense of the word. For it is exactly the people not possessing the "native tongue", thus sometimes feeling shut off from the mode of expression of native English speakers, who often make others aware of the idiomatic pitholes in the field of language: The congenitally deaf and the (foreign) learners of English [2] are the two principal target groups of idiom dictionaries. As an example of this, the first major dictionary of idioms to appear in America was published by the American School for the Deaf in 1966 [3], its second edition (1987) edited by Hungarian-born Adam Makkai, whose doctoral dissertation entitled "Idiom Structure in English" remains one of the most thorough works published on the subject.

The pervasiveness of idioms: The sky is the limit
Some linguists have claimed that any lexicalized morpheme combination with non-predictable meaning should be classified as an idiom. In this absolutist sense, not only words like *man-of-war* (warship) and *forget-me-not* (flower) should be considered idioms; words like *catgut* (string) and *parkway* (motorway) would have to be included, too. [4]

The inclusion of compound nouns like these in a dictionary of idioms would seem superfluous, though, as such words would be incorporated in any normal mono- or bilingual dictionary of English. They are fixed, easy-to-look-up lexemes, not flexible, evasive phrases with alphabetization problems. The same goes for the innumerable English phrasal verbs, as for example *put up*, *get down*, *put up with*, etc. So from a practical lexicographical point of view such units should not be designated as idioms, and hence not accepted in an idiomatic dictionary.

From an even more pragmatic angle, however, the field of idiom candidates seems almost endless: In scanning larger sequences of speech and writing one gets a clear impression that in a wider, collocational sense the idiom concept is all-pervasive. Utterances are never totally unpredictable. In verbal communication, there is limited room for improvisation; limited not only by the imagination of language users, but by the amalgamated nature of language itself. Based on his studies of large English text corpora [5], the editor in chief of the COBUILD dictionaries reached this conclusion in 1987:

> "Most normal text is made up ofy the occurrence of frequent words, and the frequent senses of less frequent words. Hence, normal text is largely delexicalized, and appears to be formed by exercise of the idiom principle, with occasional switching to the open-choice principle."
>
> "The principle of idiom is that a language user has available to him or her a large number of semi-preconstructed phrases that constitute single choices, even though they might appear to be analysable into segments." [6]

This quantum jump of the idiom concept is logical from a productive, language-encoding point of view - i.e. the approach needed when creating so-called active dictionaries. But from the receptive, decoding viewpoint, shared by lexicographers and users of "passive" dictionaries, the preconstructions truly worth the label 'idioms' will have to be the expressions which not only - to some extent - have a "pre-packaged" form, but also a non-transparent meaning.

Consequently, it is the aim of the English-Danish Idiomatic Dictionary (EDIC) to include exactly those English expressions which are at the same time fixed and opaque.

THE EDIC PRINCIPLES: CRITERIA FOR INCLUSION

Unlike most traditional monolingual dictionaries of (English) idioms, EDIC focuses on contemporary idioms in use. EDIC will cover

(condition 1) **fixed expressions** (plus spin-offs that will be recognized as such by native speakers)
(condition 2) **whose meaning cannot be deduced by means of normal** lexical and/or **grammatical** analysis, [7]
(condition 3) **documented in** British and American **standard speech and writing after 1950.** [8]

Consequently, the following types of multi-word units, though often found in traditional idiom dictionaries, will not be included in EDIC:

a) Non-metaphorical colloquial expressions (clichés): *not as young as one used to be*
b) Non-metaphorical quotations: *nature abhors a vacuum*
c) Fossilized, transparent metaphors: *join forces*

For reasons explained earlier, **another two** types of multi-word units will not be considered worthy of inclusion:

d) Simple phrasal verbs: *jack up*; *jog along*; *jump at*
e) Simple compounds: *jet set*; *juice dealer*

On the other hand, following the criteria for inclusion, certain types of multi-word units, rarely found in idiom dictionaries, will be included in EDIC:
1) Opaque slang expressions: *nine ways from breakfast*
2) Opaque exclamations: *nice going!*; *no kidding?*
3) Elliptical format phrases: *not that I'm any (better/etc)* [9]

Functional idiom categories
The idioms that are candidates for inclusion in EDIC fall into the following seven functional categories:
1) Nominal idioms: *an albatross round one's neck*
2) Adjectival idioms: *as hard as nails*
3) Verbal idioms: *feather one's nest*
4) Adverbial idioms: *by a neck*
5) Conjunctional idioms: *no thanks to*
6) Clause idioms: *no flies on somebody*
7) Sentence idioms: *the coast is clear*

THE EDIC PILOT STUDY

Based on the criteria listed above, idioms including words beginning with J and N were compiled. In this phase, all available post-war dictionaries and collections of idiomatic English usage were consulted. [10]
At a later stage, I will incorporate actual usage data from the British COBUILD corpora. A preliminary study shows a satisfying degree of correspondence between the "compilation idioms" and the "corpus idioms". [11] For this reason, I don't expect any revolutionary changes in the entries in the final version of letters J and N.

THE EDIC MICRO-STRUCTURE

Each article was designed in accordance with this pattern:

0.		HEADWORD
1.		the [idiomatic/fixed} expression
2.		Correspondent Danish expression(s)
3.		<Danish definition of the expression>
4.	A	"A usage example, preferably an authentic citation"
5.		source
6.	E	Etymological information
7.		[cross-reference]

Of this pattern, all idiom articles include lines 1, 2 and 4. Depending on the stilistic/semantic qualities of the idiom, lines 3 and 6 may be added. If an authentic example is available, line 5 is added. If the idiom in question is compared with another idiom, line 7 will be used. In the following, I will deal with the information given in each of these lines. [12]

Line 1: The expression

Although all idioms listed in EDIC are classified as fixed expressions, the individual elements are not all fixed and can be sub-classified according to their semantic status and structural variability:

Semantic status

Core elements
    1) Nuclear element
    2) Auxiliary elements
    3) Toggles (showing interchangeability within a closed class)
    4) Jokers (showing interchangeability within an open class) [13]

Peripheral elements
    5) Optional elements (which may be added to the core)

Structural variability
A) Fixed form
B) Flexible form (prone to inflection etc.)

Whereas categories (1) through (5) place the idiom constituents at a certain distance from the semantic center of the idiom, categories (A) and (B) deal with grammatical interdependence between the elements.
In looking at the way an idiom is presented in EDIC, the reader is able to identify the status and variability of each constituent, thus gaining information as to how to put the idiom into active use.
This labeling is expressed by means of certain graphic codes:

bold underline, element also found as headword	: status (1) A or B
bold underline, non-marked	: status (2) A or B
bold underline within ( )-brackets	: status (5) A or B
bold underline within { }-brackets	: status (3) A or B
underline	: status (4) B
asterisk *	: status B
no asterisk	: status A

With this system of notation, the formulation
{put*/have*/get*} one's nose* (down) to the grindstone
refers to possible usage ranging from "Jack Yablonski kept his nose to the grindstone during those critical months" to "We're putting our noses down to the grindstone, Sir!"
The EDIC notation makes it easy to distinguish between for example the pronominal variability in expressions such as
1) **_before you can* say Jack Robinson_** and
2) **_have* one's nose in a book_**.
While (1) accepts only the general "you", (2) takes all pronouns.

Line 2: The Danish equivalents
As the purpose of the EDIC project is to create a dictionary of actual usage ('parole') more than potential constructions ('langue'), this line includes not simply one or several possible multi-word units that structurally resemble the source language expression, but rather a cluster of semantically and pragmatically acceptable translations, i.e. those expressions that are the most likely to be found in Danish speech and writing.
In classifying these Danish equivalents [14], one must operate with at least five categories:

A. *Twins*
Seemingly in contradiction with the commonly held belief that idioms are the very lexical units least expected to have a word-for-word-equivalent in foreign languages, English idioms quite often have well-established counterparts in Danish. Of course, a lot of such pairs - as *nothing new under the sun* vs. *intet nyt under solen*, which both originate from the Bible - have come into use independently in the two languages.

B. *Calques*
But in a number of cases, (newer) English idioms as *in full swing, up to sb* (somebody) and the very frequent *skeleton* in the closet/cupboard* have coined Danish calques: *i fuldt sving, op til nn* (nogen) and *skeletter i skabet* are now fully naturalized, the latter idiom even in the process of ousting the original Danish equivalent *lig i lasten* (corpses in the cargo).

C. *Parallels*
With two cultures as closely related as the Anglo-Saxon and the Scandinavian, idiomatic expressions in Danish will often resemble their English counterparts. Apart from this, many idioms are centered around elements common to mankind: the different parts of the human body, basic facts of nature etc. One example will suffice: *feather* one's own nest* is

equivalent to the Danish idiom *mele* sin egen kage* (flour one's own cake) in both construction and meaning.

D. Paraphrases
In semantic slots where no idioms are available in Danish, other constructions are used, whether we deal with translations or original Danish discourse. The most common of these alternatives, truly idiomatic in the 'loyal-to-the-vernacular' sense, is a paraphrase. When Danes want to express the meaning found in *not have* a hair to one's name* they will use the expression *ikke have* et hår på hovedet* (not have a hair on one's head) or *være* pilskaldet* (be as bald as an egg).

E.. Single-word-lexemes
In a few cases, a semantic slot occupied by an English idiom is filled by a Danish compound, as with the simile *as nervous as a {cat/kitten}*. The corresponding Danish word here is *hunderæd* (dog-scared).

Line 3: Danish definition
If the cluster of Danish correspondents does not include an expression that unequivocally explains the meaning of the idiom, a literal definition will be added. Thus, the expression *set* one's jaw**, its prime Danish equivalents being *bide* tænderne sammen* (press together one's teeth), is supplied with this definition: <anstrenge sig for ikke at lide nederlag> (act with the determination not to be defeated).

Lines 4 and 5: Usage example, and source
In the pilot study, these examples are taken from existing dictionaries or from my own observations of English in use. Most of the examples are authentic, but some of the dictionary examples are clearly invented. In a few cases, no examples have been found at this stage.
Most of the authentic examples, which are always cited in context, come

from written sources, mainly fiction. However, newspapers, film and television have also contributed with a number of citations. For instance, the example following the idiom *no dice* is a stretch of film dialog: "When I asked for a room he immediately said no dice." The source is listed as "episode of the TV series Hill Street Blues, USA 1983." A more "literary" idiom may be illustrated by a book citation. Thus, *turn* over a new leaf* is exemplified by the quotation "It is due to his protection and advice that I remained at Sandhurst, turned over a new leaf, and survived to make good". Here the source line states: "The Memoirs of Field-Marshal Montgomery (1958)".

A typical "lexicographer's own blend" example is found with the idiom *go* by the name of...* : "This wild flower goes by the name of Old Man's Beard." In the pilot phase, this was one of the idioms with no authentic quotations available.

Line 6: Etymology

In idioms such as *not know* where one's next penny is coming from*, the transition from literary to metaphorical meaning is easy to understand. Here, etymological information will be limited to data determining the age of the idiomatic use of the phrase. Expressions as *talk* nineteen to the dozen* remain opaque, even after they have been detected as idioms. In such cases, more elaborate data will be provided, if available. But, with idioms of this type, the etymological information found in existing dictionaries often seem a far cry from being accurate, let alone reliable. In a number of instances, different lexicographical authories contradict one another.

As to the origins of the idiom *dressed (up) to the nines*, at least three different explanations circulate:

a) The modern expression is a distortion of *to then eyne*, in present-day English: *to the eyes*. (Brewer's Dictionary of Phrase and Fable)

b) The expression refers to the Oriental belief in the magic qualities of the number 9, representing a trinity of trinities. (A Concise Dictionary of

English Idioms)
c) The phrase refers to the Western habit of rating certain qualities on a scale from one to ten, a score of nine thus seen as high. (Longman Dictionary of English Idioms)

In such instances I shall refrain from interpreting the etymology of the idiom in question. After all, no information is preferable to dubious information. But, of course, when the available information seems reliable, it is included.

Thus, the article on *feather* one's (own) nest** has: Registered from 1553. Used by the poet Robert Greene in 1590: "She sees thou has fethred thy nest, and hast crowns in thy purse".

An expression of modern origin, *{carry*/etc} coals to Newcastle*, receives the following comment: Refers to Newcastle-upon-Tyne, formerly the center of the coal-mining English industry.

An American English idiomatic calque, *{need*/want*} sth like (one {needs*/wants*}) a hole in the head*, is supplied with this etymological information: From Yiddish *loch in kop*. Common British usage since c. 1950.

Line 7: Cross-references
References between articles are shown as in this example: [see also: *a rose by any other name would smell as sweet*]. This cross-reference, i.e. reference from article to article, as opposed to references from non-article to an article, [15] is found in line seven of the article *what's in a name?*.

MACRO-STRUCTURE IN IDIOMATIC DICTIONARIES

Different approaches to alphabetization and references
A single-word oriented dictionary, whether monolingual or bilingual, simply lists its lexemes alphabetically. The only major problem is then to decide either to adopt the principle recommended by e.g. the Danish Standards

Association (an organ for establishing industrial and terminological norms) or the traditional principle followed by most dictionary makers. [16]. In single-word dictionaries, fixed phrases are almost always included as run-on entries only. They are treated under the headword considered most central by the lexicographers.

Within the field of multi-word lexicography, we can observe five different types of macro-structure:

1) A **thesaurus** system, whereby lexically related idioms are grouped around a limited number of keywords.

    In the "Penguin Dictionary of English Idioms", these keywords are then in turn listed non-alphabetically, in chapters. This means that for instance the idiom *before one could say Jack Robinson* is grouped with thirteen other idioms around an entry called BOY'S NAMES: JACK in a chapter (out of 33) called THE HOUSE. In this chapter, the fourteen "Jack-idioms" and the other "boys' names-idioms" are found before both GIRLS' NAMES and BIBLICAL NAMES (!)

2) A **conceptual** system, whereby functionally related idioms are grouped together. Thus, in "Using Idioms" (Prentice Hall), under the keyword SPEED we find *before you could say Jack Robinson/in the twinkling of an eye*.

3) A **grammatical** system, grouping idioms which are structurally related. In Seidl & McMordie's "English Idioms" expressions of the type *before you could say Jack Robinson* are classified as 'Idioms with prepositions' and arranged alphabetically.

4) An **alpha-lexical** system, whereby lexically related idioms are grouped under alphabetically listed keywords. Having this structure, the "Longman Dictionary of English Idioms" places *before one/you can/could say Jack Robinson* under JACK, found as the first keyword under the letter J.

5) A purely **alphabetical** system, used by e.g. the "Dictionary of American Idioms". From 'Jack Robinson' the reader is referred to the article

under the letter B: *before one can say Jack Robinson.*

The same strictly alphabetical principle is found in the two-volume "Oxford Dictionary of Current Idiomatic English", by far the most comprehensive work of English idioms, American or British. Finding an idiom like *before you can say Jack Robinson* in this dictionary (hereafter referred to as ODCIE) is quite easy for the reader.

However, adhering to the alphabetization principle without any use of references, the policy followed in ODCIE, may prove to be disastrous in some instances. The next paragraph will illustrate this.

The maze of alphabetization: an example

When searching in the ODCIE for an expression such as *get no change out of*, the average dictionary user runs into severe problems. With access to both volumes, the user first has to decide which one to turn to. Should he consult "Volume 1: Phrasal Verbs", or "Volume 2: English Idioms"? In the latter - and newer - volume he finds idioms such as *get uptight (about sth)* and *get a slap in the face*, but not the expression he wants. Deciding, then, that the wanted idiom may be considered more of a phrasal verb than the two expressions he did find, our user turns to volume 1. Checking the index this time, to make sure that the wanted idiom is in the book, he is happy to note that under the headword 'change/changes' the index says: 'get no ~ out of'. But no page is given. Recognizing the alphabetical principle, he then expects to find his idiom between *get into one's stride* and *get one's teeth into*. No luck.

He makes a second attempt: This time he looks between *get by on/upon* and *get down*, because maybe 'no change' will be treated as simply 'change'. Still no luck!

If our average dictionary user has had the time and courage to read the 80 page long (!) front matter, he may have learned that the expression will be alphabetized as if it had been spelled 'get out of no change'.

So the well-above-average user makes a third attempt: He concentrates on a point between *get blood out of a stone* and *get out of one's depth*, totally convinced that since in the alphabet 'blood' precedes both 'no' and 'change' with 'one's' placed after 'no', he has now hacked his way into the secret compartment where the Oxford lexicographers hide "his" idiom. But, alas, the wanted expression is just not there. Only by making a fourth try, searching between *get a kick out of* and *get out of somebody's sight*, does he succeed. The explanation lies in the fact that 'one's' is ignored in the ODCIE alphabetization of *get out of one's depth* from his previous search. Since, alphabetically, 'no' comes after 'depth', the wanted expression ends up in its place at page 122. Voilà!

THE EDIC MACRO-STRUCTURE

References

The English-Danish Idiomatic Dictionary prefers too many references to too many frustrated readers: A little extra work for the dictionary maker, but a large help for the dictionary user.

But on the other hand, we do not want to take it to extremes: Unlike some reference books which present the same article at different places (thus appearing impressive and bulky) the EDIC will simply direct the reader to the right headword from all relevant corners. Two examples will suffice:

1) Under the headwords CUT, SPITE and FACE the EDIC user will find, locally alphabetized, the message "< cut* off one's **nose*** to spite one's face*". This reference tells the reader to look for the expression at the alphabetical place of the highlighted headword, in this case: NOSE.

2) In cases where the desired idiom is treated by the EDIC as a variant form, the central idiom is referred to in this way: "< put* one's foot in a wasp's nest: stir* up a **hornets'** nest". This reference is found under PUT, FOOT, WASP and NEST. In the same way, the message "< bring* a hornets' nest about one's ears: stir* up a **hornets'** nest" is found under BRING, NEST and EARS.

Arrangement of entries

The EDIC is arranged alpha-lexically, with strict alphabetization within keywords only. This, together with the generous use of references, accounts for a sequence of entries as the following, taken from NECK in version 1 of the pilot study: [17]

a millstone round one's {head/neck}
< a **pain** in the neck
an albatross round one's neck
be* breaking one's neck for sth
< be* neck and neck: **neck** and neck
be* up to {the/one's} neck in sth
< bone-headed from the neck up: **dead** from the neck up
break* one's neck {doing sth/trying to do sth}
breathe* down {one's/sb's} neck
by a (short) neck
< catch* it in the neck: get* it in the **neck**
< chance* one's neck: risk one's **neck**
< **dead** from the neck up
{down/on} {one's/sb's} neck*
fall* on sb's neck
get* it in {the/one's} neck
< get* off {one's/sb's} neck: get* off {one's/sb's} **back**
give* (one's) neck
< have* a neck (to do sth): have* the **nerve** (to do sth)
< have* **eyes** {at/in} the back of one's {head/neck}
have* sth (hanging) {around/round} one's neck
(in {this/your/etc}) neck of the woods
< lose* by a neck: by a **neck**
neck and crop
neck and neck (with {sb/sth})

neck or nothing
risk* one's neck*
save* {one/sb's} neck*
{stick*/stretch} one's neck* out
< talk* {out of/through the back of} one's neck*:
    talk* out of the **top** of one's head*
< throw*/kick*} sb out on {his/her/their} neck*: on sb's **ear**
< {throw*/turn*} sb out neck and crop: **neck** and crop
< win* by a neck: by a **neck**

As exemplified in the last line, the EDIC even operates with references within headwords. With NECK covering three pages in version 1, this practice facilitates the retrieval of the expression searched for.

Following the alpha-lexical principle, an idiom such as *not a moment too soon* (for this purpose dubbed type 1) is placed under NOT, whereas *not have* a leg to stand on* (type 2) is referred to the keyword LEG. The reason for this discrimination is the fact that with type 1, 'not' is not syntactically eroded in use, as opposed to the weaker 'not' in the type 2 idiom: Whereas "she arrived not a moment too soon" is good English, "she didn't arrive a moment too soon" is unidiomatic - in several senses of this word. Conversely, "she didn't have a leg to stand on" is idiomatic, while "she had not a leg to stand on" is not. By not observing this distinction, strictly alphabetical works like the ODCIE show a tendency of heavy accumulation of entries around semantically or structurally weak words like 'be','have', 'in', 'take' and - as expected - 'not'. No less than 103 out of ODCIE's 263 N-idioms turn out to be phrases beginning with 'not'.

In comparison, of EDIC's 247 idioms including the element 'not', only in the 62 cases where the word 'not' retains its full syntactic status is that idiom treated under NOT. The 185 type 2 idioms are referred to keywords elsewhere in the alphabet.

SIZE AND SCOPE OF EDIC

Size
In a one-column layout, the two specimen letters, J and N, reach a count of 15 and 64 A4 pages respectively.
In monolingual English idiomatic dictionaries of a similar (alpha-lexical) macro-structure, letter J takes up about 1% and N about 4% of the total dictionary, front and back matter not included. In its pre-corpora shape, with letters J and N representing 5% of the dictionary proper, the English-Danish Idiomatic Dictionary will reach a count of 1,600 A4 pages. The specimen letters occupy a total of 234 kilobytes in the word processor, equaling 2,950 characters per page.
With a layout as compressed as the one used in the ODCIE, cramming two columns with 3,150 characters each into every page, the book version of the EDIC will cover approximately 800 pages. In comparison, volume 2 of the ODCIE takes up 606 pages.

Scope
Also in terms of scope, i.e. the number of entries, the EDIC will place itself well above the standard idiomatic dictionary of English: Letter J treats 115 idioms, while 64 idioms are referred to keywords with other initials than J, and 1 idiom is referred from one possible J keyword to another. Letter N treats 497 idioms and refers 468 idioms, of which 93 are referred to another N keyword.
In comparison, the (alpha-lexical) "Longman Dictionary of English Idioms" treats 125 N-idioms and refers 134 idioms, while the ODCIE, vol. 2, treats 263. As mentioned earlier, due to its macro-structure, this dictionary refers none.
The total number of idioms included in volume 2 of the Oxford dictionary is around 7,000, whereas the Longman dictionary reaches a figure of some 4,500. Judging from the scope of the two specimen letters, and considering

the EDIC macro-structure, the expected number of entries in EDIC will be around 12,000.

NOTES

[1] The third of these senses is of course the most commonly used nowadays. In this sense of the word, 'idiom' is defined by the Collins English Dictionary (1989) as: "a group of words whose meaning cannot be predicted from the meanings of the constituent words, as for example *(It was raining) cats and dogs*".
On the other side of the Atlantic, Webster's Ninth New Collegiate Dictionary (1990) suggests a wider definition for this sense of 'idiom': "an expression in the usage of a language that is peculiar to itself either grammatically (as *no, it wasn't me*) or in having a meaning that cannot be derived from the conjoined meanings of its elements (as *Monday week* for 'the Monday a week after next Monday'."

[2] Of course, the natural learners of English, children, act as an important litmus test of the idiomaticity of a certain phrase. However, idioms are rarely focused on in children's dictionaries.

[3] In Denmark, the first dictionary of Danish idioms ever, due late 1992, is a product of the efforts of teaching for immigrants and refugees. In Britain, with its 'English for Foreign Learners' tradition, almost all idiom dictionaries are aimed at non-native speakers.

[4] Charles F. Hockett considers such monomorphemic utterances idioms. As an example, a 'cupboard' is not (nowadays) a board for cups. (See Hockett 1958)

[5] By late 1991, four such corpora, totaling 44.3 million running words, were established:
a) "Twenty", with 18 million words, mainly from written post-war fiction, British and American. This main corpus formed the database of the 1987 "Collins COBUILD English Language Dictionary".
b) "BBC World Service", with 20 million words, all from radio and television broadcasts, mostly news stories based on written manuscripts.

c) "Times", a newspaper corpus consisting of the entire text of the London Times through 18 months in 1989-1990.

d) "Spoken", consisting of 1.3 million randomly collected words of spoken conversation recorded in the 1980'es among well-educated Britons.

[6] Sinclair 1991, pp. 113 and 110, respectively.

[7] By 'normal' analysis I mean the result of decoding by 'naive' speakers/readers of English, including children and foreign learners of English.

[8] I will define standard speech as linguistic phenomena familiar to an educated native speaker; phenomena which may or may not be used by the speaker personally. Expressions only known in particular niches of society, such as professional jargon, etc, are considered non-standard.

[9] For the term 'format phrases' I am indebted to Nigel Rees. (See Rees 1990, vii-viii.)

[10] In my bibliography, these works are listed independently.

[11] See Gottlieb (forthcoming).

[12] By 'line' I mean a typographically marked paragraph of an EDIC article, no matter the actual number of lines used.

[13] The element *one's*, although representing a limited number of lexical items (the English possessive pronouns) is placed in this category, together with elements such as *sb's*, which represent an unlimited number of items (all animate nouns in the genitive).

[14] Defined as 'functionally corresponding expressions', cf. Nida's concept of 'functional equivalence' (see Nida & de Waard 1986).

[15] Such references, leading the dictionary user to the article of interest, i.e. the alphabetical location of a certain idiomatic phrase, are dealt with in the following chapter, "Macro-structure".

[16] According to the former principle, 'ad lib' will be placed between 'ad hoc' and 'adjourn': Word-dividing space is considered alphabetically

relevant. Conforming to the latter principle, 'adjourn' will be alphabetized between the two-word entries: Only the alpha-numerical characters count.

[15] In version 2, now in preparation, all entries will be tried against corpus evidence, and only authentic examples will be accepted.

BIBLIOGRAPHY

References, alphabetically listed

Boatner, M.T.; J.E. Gates & A. Makkai
   A Dictionary of American Idioms
   American School for the Deaf 1966
Collins English Dictionary
   Collins, Birmingham 1989
Gottlieb, Henrik
   Idioms in Corpora: Types, Tokens, Frequencies and Lexicographical Implications
   in: Proceedings from the Sixth International Symposium on Lexicography, University of Copenhagen May 7-9, 1992
   Gunter Narr, Tübingen, Series Maior (forthcoming)
Hockett, Charles F.
   A Course in Modern Linguistics - MacMillan, New York 1958
Landau, Sidney I.
   Dictionaries: The Art and Craft of Lexicography
   Charles Scribner's Sons, New York 1984
Makkai, Adam
   Idiom Structure in English - Mouton, The Hague/Paris 1972
Michelsen, Christian
   Dansk Idiomordbog - Gyldendal, Copenhagen (forthcoming)
Nida, Eugene A., & J. de Waard
   From one Language to Another - Thomas Nelson Publishers, Nashville 1986
Rees, Nigel
   A Dictionary of Popular Phrases - Bloomsbury, London 1990
Sinclair, John M.
   Corpus, Concordance, Collocation - Oxford University Press 1991

Birmingham 1987
Webster's Ninth Collegiate Dictionary
Merriam-Webster, Springfield, Massachusetts 1990

Dictionaries of English Idioms, semi-chronologically listed:

A Dictionary of English Idioms, part II: Colloquial Phrases
B.L.K. & G.O.E. Henderson, James Blackwood 1950
A Book of English Idioms
V.H. Collins, Longmans 1956
A Second Book of English Idioms
V.H. Collins, Longmans 1958
A Third Book of English Idioms
V.H. Collins, Longmans 1960
The Kenkyusha Dictionary of Current English Idioms
Sanki Ichiwaka et alias, Kenkyusha (Tokyo) 1964
A Concise Dictionary of English Idioms
William Freeman & B.A. Phythian, 3rd edition,
Hodder and Stoughton 1973
(Original edition: William Freeman 1951)
Handbook of American Idioms and Idiomatic Usage
Harold C. Whitford & Robert J. Dixson, Regents Publishing 1973
(Original edition: Whitford & Dixson 1953)
Oxford Dictionary of Current Idiomatic English
Volume 1: *Verbs with Prepositions & Particles*
A.P. Cowie & R. Mackin, Oxford University Press 1975
Volume 2: *Phrase, Clause and Sentence Idioms*
A.P. Cowie, R. Mackin & I.R. McCaig, Oxford Univ. Press 1983
Dictionary of English Colloquial Idioms
Frederick T. Wood & Robert J. Hill, rev. edition, Macmillan 1979
(Original edition: Frederick T. Wood 1969)

Longman Dictionary of English Idioms
   Thomas Hill Long & Della Summers, Longman 1979
Longman Dictionary of Phrasal Verbs
   Rosemary Courtney, Longman 1983
Chambers Idioms
   E.M. Kirkpatrick & C.M. Schwarz, Chambers 1982
A Dictionary of Contemporary Idioms
   Martin H. Manser, Pan Books 1983
A Learner's Dictionary of English Idioms
   Isabel McCaig & Martin H. Manser, Oxford University Press 1986
The Penguin Dictionary of English Idioms
   Daphne M. Gulland & David G. Hinds-Howell, Penguin Books 1986
A Dictionary of American Idioms
   Adam Makkai 1987
   (Original edition: M.T. Boatner, J.E. Gates & A. Makkai 1966)
NTC's American Idioms Dictionary
   Richard A. Spears & Linda Schinke-Llano
   National Textbook Company 1987
English Idioms
   Jennifer Seidl & W. McMordie, fifth edition, Oxford Univ. Press 1988
   (Original edition: W. McMordie 1909)
Harrap's Dictionary of English Idioms
   John O.E. Clark, Harrap Books 1990

Other sources, alphabetically listed according to title:

1000 aktuelle talemåder på dansk, engelsk og tysk
   Viggo Jensen - Chr. Erichsen, Copenhagen 1982
20,000 Proverbs
   - and their equivalents in German, French, Swedish, Danish
   Jens Aa. Stabell Bilgrav - Hans Heide Publishing, Copenhagen 1985

A Hog on Ice - and Other Curious Expressions
   Charles Earl Funk - New York 1948
Amerikansk-dansk slangordbog
   Kris Winther (translated into Danish by Marianne Holmen)
   Hans Reitzels Forlag, Copenhagen 1984
   (Swedish editions: Kris Winther 1970 and 1979)
Bevingede Ord
   T. Vogel-Jørgensen og Poul Zerlang - G.E.C. Gad, Copenhagen 1990
BBI Combinatory Dictionary of English
   Morton Benson, Evelyn Benson & Robert Ilson - John Benjamins 1986
Brewer's Dictionary of Phrase and Fable, seventh edition
   E. Cobham Brewer - London 1981
   (Original edition: E. Cobham Brewer 1870)
Collins COBUILD English Language Dictionary
   John M. Sinclair et alias - Collins 1987
Concise Dictionary of Slang and Unconventional English
   Paul Beale & Eric Partridge - Routledge 1989
   (Original unabridged edition: Eric Partridge 1961)
Dictionary of Catch Phrases
   Eric Partridge - Routledge and Kegan Paul 1977
Dictionary of Contemporary Slang
   Jonathan Green - Pan Books 1984
Engelsk-Dansk Ordbog
   B. Kjærulff-Nielsen - Gyldendal, Copenhagen 1989
Englische Idiomatik - Nachschlagewerk der Englische Umgangssprache
   R. Mar-Osterford - Max Hueber Verlag, Munich 1956
Everyday English Phrases, Their Idiomatic Meanings and Origins
   J.S. Whitehead - London 1937
Everyman's Modern Phrase and Fable
   Gyles Brandreth - London 1990

Lexicographic Description of English
    Morton Benson, Evelyn Benson & Robert Ilson - John Benjamins 1986
New Dictionary of American Slang
    Robert L. Chapman - Harper & Row 1986
Ord och inga visor - 2000 svenska idiom i engelsk översättning
    Lars Hübinette & Bengt Odenstedt - Studentlitteratur, Lund 1988
Phrase and Word Origins
    Alfred H. Holt - New York 1961
Practical Guide to Colloquial Idiom
    W.J. Ball - London 1958
Rockspeak! The Dictionary of Rock Terms
    Tom Hibbert - Omnibus Press 1983
Say "Uncle!" - Amerikanske talemåder
    Martha Gaylord - P. Haase & Søn, Copenhagen 1950
Say When - og 1284 andre engelske talemåder og udtryk
    Marianne Holmen - Høst og Søn, Copenhagen 1990
U.S.A.-Slang. Ordbog over moderne, amerikansk slang
    Victor Skaarup og Kris Winther - Commodore, Copenhagen 1946

APPENDIX: Examples of EDIC articles

NOSE
cut* off one's nose to spite one's face
    gøre* sig selv en bjørnetjeneste, gøre* det værst for sig selv, pisse* i bukserne for at få varmen, save* sin egen gren over, stikke* hovedet i busken
    <bedrage sig selv>
A "And so there's a limit to the extent to which this confrontation can really be carried forward. Okay, you can cut off your nose to spite your face and get away with it for a bit, but in the end you have to come to the reality."
    Sir Guy Huntrods, Lloyd's Bank International, i BBC Channel Four: A Matter of Life and Debt, part III (1987)
E Betydningsbaggrund: skærer man sin (grimme) næse af, bliver man endnu grimmere.

JUST
({it/that} is*) just {one's/sb's} luck!
    det skulle lige passe, (det var*) lige det der manglede, selvfølgelig!
A "Saturday night, no place to go,
    Just sittin' round and feelin' low
    Worked hard all week to make a buck,
    My girl's got a headache, just my luck!
    Mrozinski Brothers: "Polka Shoes" (amerikansk popsang) ca. 1980
E Fast ironisk udtryk.

Jørgen Erik Nielsen

DICKENSIAN NEOLOGISMS
AS POSSIBLE SOURCES OF DANISH NEOLOGISMS

Linguistic studies of an author's work may help us to appreciate why he or she attained his or her literary position; or they can open a possibility for us, though necessarily an imperfect one, to read the author as contemporary readers did; or they can give us some idea of the difficulties that the author's translators have been up against. The aim of the present paper is to examine to what extent translations of neologisms in the source language have given rise to neologisms in the target language, in this case Danish. We shall not be primarily concerned with translators' tribulations, but with neologisms that did or did not give rise to new formations in Danish. The basic assumption is that the translator came across a brand new word, meaning or phrase, which no dictionary at his disposal could possibly contain; he came up with a translation, coining a Danish neologism, which later appeared in dictionaries.

The validity of that assumption will be tested here on some Dickens translations. Dickens's novels were translated into Danish immediately after the appearance of the originals, consequently neologisms, or at least brand new words or phrases appearing in them, must have been almost equally new when they met the first translator's eye. Further, the popularity of Dickens translations in Denmark makes it reasonable to assume that a neologism appearing in one of them will have been read by a large public. Finally, we have easy access to Dickensian neologisms, as Professor Knud Sørensen has in his book **Charles Dickens: Linguistic Innovator** (Aarhus, 1985) in an appendix assembled a long list of such neologisms (pp. 115-169). Most of them have been established as neologisms on the authority of the **Oxford English Dictionary** (the **OED**), but he includes a number of words, meanings and phrases that have been overlooked by the dictionary. "Dickensian neologism" in Professor Sørensen's book and consequently in the present article is a word, meaning or phrase whose first recorded appearance is a work by Dickens. We can never be absolutely certain that the neologism was actually coined by him, but even if somebody else should have been the first to use the term, it seems certain that it was quite new when Dickens used it. Professor Sørensen has in some cases been able to antedate some of the earliest appearances recorded in the **OED,** still he says that "it seems reasonable to subscribe to the observation made by John Algeo: 'it is likely in most cases that the earliest date given by the OED is close to the initial appearance of the word in English'"(p.27). So much for our possibilities of determining the "birthday" of an English word or phrase; are we in a position to establish with any degree of certainty the earliest appearance of a Danish word? In the introduction by Lis Jacobsen and H. Juul-Jensen to vol. I (Copenhagen, 1919) of **Ordbog over det danske Sprog** (the **ODS**), the two lexicographers state categorically that there is no telling whether the earliest appearance of a word or meaning has been recorded by the dictionary (pp. XLV-XLVI). Still, an old lexicographer on the staff of the **ODS**, which registers the Danish vocabulary on the basis of material printed after 1699, has told me that 18th-century appearances of words and meanings were always included if such had been registered; further, the staff of the forthcoming supplement volumes have kindly allowed me to search their collections for possible examples antedating first-appearances registered in the dictionary; so we shall for our purpose use the **ODS** (i.e. the dictionary and the material for the supplement) as furnishing reliable evidence of, at least, early appearances of words and meanings. Three bilingual dictionaries have been used to see if neologisms from translations found their way into them, viz. the three biggest English-Danish dictionaries from the middle of the 19th century till the present day: Svend Rosing's **Engelsk-Dansk Ordbog**, the 6th edition (Copenhagen, 1887), whose first edition had appeared in 1853; J. Brynildsen's **Engelsk-dansk-norsk Ordbog**, vol.I-II (Copenhagen, 1902-1907); and B. Kjærulff Nielsen's **Engelsk-dansk Ordbog**, 2nd edition (Copenhagen, 1981), whose first edition had appeared in 1964. Rosing worked out and revised his dictionary contemporarily with the appearance of the early Dickens translations, Brynildsen composed *his* work when Dickens's works had become classics and with occasional special reference to him as to other English authors; and Kjærulff Nielsen's dictionary belongs to our own days and can, hopefully, tell us whether a neologism has survived or not.

It is fairly easy to be struck by certain odd expressions or words in Dickens, like "Circumlocution Office" in **Little Dorrit** or "gunpowderous" in **The Mystery of Edwin Drood**; it is more surprising to read in Knud Sørensen's book that "casualty ward" (in **Sketches by Boz**, ch. VI, "The Hospital Patient", p.242)[1] and "allotment garden" (in **The Uncommercial Traveller**, ch.XXIV, "An Old Stage-coaching House", p.247) are Dickensian neologisms too. The two first words are humorous terms, whereas the two others have become part and parcel of "ordinary" English. Have those four Dickensian neologisms given rise to Danish neologisms?

"The Circumlocution Office", which is frequently mentioned in **Little Dorrit** (1855-57), was by Moltke (1856) translated into "Omsvøbsdepartementet", which word has been recorded by the **ODS** with reference both to Moltke's translation of Dickens's novel and to a Danish newspaper (1906), where the word is used without any reference to Dickens. Interestingly, among the examples of the supplement material there is an early similar one from a newspaper in 1858, in which "kommunale Omsvøbsdepartementer" ("local Circumlocution Offices") are mentioned; somebody must immediately have grasped the possibilities of that new humorous derogatory word. In this case the Dickensian neologism did give rise to a Danish one. "Omsvøbsdepartementet" has been preserved as *the* Danish term in Eva Hemmer Hansen's modern translation of **Little Dorrit** (1975), and it is given as the Danish equivalent of "the Circumlocution Office" by Brynildsen and Kjærulff Nielsen, but not registered by Rosing.

The adjective "gunpowderous", which appears in **The Mystery of Edwin Drood (1870)**, ch. 6, p. 57, where we are told about Mr. Honeythunder that "his philanthropy was of that gunpowderous sort that the difference between it and animosity was hard to determine," is clearly a humorously meant word, but probably a nonce-word. It was by Moltke (1870) translated into "voldsom", i.e. "violent", and thus without any attempt to coin an unusual equivalent, and that survived the 1894 revision of this translation. Eva Hemmer Hansen translates it into "ukrudtsagtig", i.e. "like weeds" (1985), a word that may in the context possess some of the humorous flavour of "gunpowderous", but which is not felt as a particularly strange formation, though it is not in the **ODS**. As might be expected, "gunpowderous" is not found in the three English-Danish dictionaries. The compound "casualty ward" first appeared in **Sketches by Boz** (1836-7); in an anonymous translation of that sketch in the periodical **Almue-Vennen**, No. 1, 2-1-1842 (Århus) we find for "casualty ward" the Danish word "værelse", whereas Moltke in his translation of the entire book (1856) says "stue"; both words correspond to "room", thus there is no attempt made to find or coin a more specialised term. Rosing does not register "casualty ward", Brynildsen translates it by "modtagelsesstue" (the reception of the hospital), Kjærulff Nielsen says that it corresponds to "skadestue" (the ward in the hospital where accidents are treated), which word is recorded by the **ODS** only from 1908 (on the basis of a telephone directory). The chapter in **The Uncommercial Traveller** containing the neologism "allotment garden" first appeared in **All the Year Round** in 1863; apparently it was not translated till 1969 (by C.A.Bodelsen in Charles Dickens, **Natterejse til Calais og andre essays**), by which time the Danish equivalent "kolonihave", used by

Bodelsen in his translation, had been long established in Danish (the earliest recorded example in the **ODS** is from 1901; an older word was "arbejderhave", i.e. "worker's garden"); of the English-Danish dictionaries examined, only Kjærulff Nielsen registers "allotment garden", which he translates by "havelod, kolonihave." So the result of our investigation of the four Dickensian neologisms is that only "Circumlocution Office", gave rise to a Danish neologism, but a word that is used both in translations of **Little Dorrit** and as a word in its own right.

In order to establish whether that result is characteristic of the treatment of Dickensian neologisms in Danish, I have tried from Sørensen's list to pick out all neologisms in **Great Expectations**, which appeared in 1860-1 (Sørensen has found 35 of them), and see how they have been treated by Danish translators and lexicographers. **Great Expectations** appeared in Danish translation by Moltke in 1861, which translation was revised in 1894. The modern translation by Eva Hemmer Hansen appeared in 1982. A heavily, but skilfully abridged translation by Julie Meyn from 1896 has only contributed a few words to the present study. There is no reason to keep the reader on tenterhooks: The examination of that material, much larger than the four examples discussed above, has not provided us with clear instances of Danish neologisms having been created thanks to the impact of Dickens translations. Why are our results so meagre?

For one thing, our use of the term "Dickensian neologism" in a wide sense leads to the inclusion of examples where we cannot possibly tell whether the Danish equivalents in translations and dictionaries are neologisms or not. Thus the collocation "aged parent", used by Wemmick about his father, is included in the list; Moltke has "alderstegen fader", Meyn "gamling" and Hemmer Hansen "alderstegent ophav"; the English collocation is not in the English-Danish dictionaries, and we have no possibility of determining through the **ODS** whether any of the Danish ones might here have appeared for the first time; "gamling" certainly is not a neologism (recorded by the **ODS** from 1801). Among the Dickensian neologisms we also find the adverb "buzzingly": ".., the pupils formed in a line and buzzingly passed a ragged book from hand to hand" (ch.X, p.68). Moltke has "mumlende" and Hemmer Hansen "højt snakkende", but the present participle of a Danish verb is uninflected, makes no formal distinction between adjective and adverb. The adjective "peppercorny", used about Mr. Pumblechook's premises (ch.VIII, p.49), is by both Moltke and Hemmer Hansen translated by "peberkornet", and Moltke's use of the word may well be the first time in Danish considering its unusual character; the word is in neither the **ODS** nor the three English-Danish dictionaries, so even if Moltke here used the word for the first time in Danish, he did not create a word with an existence outside the bounds of his translation. Another word in the novel that is clearly a nonce-word, is the verb "to nutcracker": "Are infants to be nutcrackered into their tombs, and is nobody to save them?" (ch.XXIII, p.183). Hemmer Hansen coins the similar verb "nøddeknækkereres", which, not surprisingly, we look in vain for in the dictionaries. It may have appeared here for the first time in Danish, but so far for the last time too.

One of the nominalised phrasal verbs listed by Bent Nordhjem in his article in the present volume, "kick-up", is a neologism: "An ox vanished with a kick-up of his hind-legs and a flourish of his tail" (ch.III, p.14). Moltke and Hemmer Hansen both use verb-phrases, Rosing and Brynildsen do not register the noun in the literal sense, and Kjærulff Nielsen gives an explanation. Clearly, nothing new has been added to the Danish vocabulary; that nobody has attempted to calque the English word is what we might expect, as Nordhjem makes it clear that the NPV is not a productive type of noun-formation in Danish.

Dickens introduced "commercial" as a sort of abbreviation for "commercial traveller" (ch. XIII, p. 99). Moltke and Hemmer Hansen, Brynildsen and

Kjærulff Nielsen all translate that by "handelsrejsende", which was a fairly new word (and profession?) then, replacing "agent" and later being partly replaced by "repræsentant". The earliest appearance of "handelsrejsende" in the **ODS** is from 1850 in Søren Kierkegaard's **Indøvelse i Christendom**, but it may be too fanciful to suggest that Moltke, when he was translating **Great Expectations** a decade later, picked on the modern word because he realized that Dickens's choice was here new and unconventional.

It will be obvious to the reader by now that many of the "new terms" discussed here are nonce-words or terms with special, unusual connotations, dispensible if you take an interest merely in the denotations of the words. Dickens is not Dickens without all the connotations, but undoubtedly in many cases the translator did not know that the word to be translated was a new coinage. The jocularly old-fashioned flavour of "asmear" in "all asmear with filth and fat and blood and foam" (ch.20, p. 155) is lost in Moltke's "tilsølet", i.e. "soiled", and the old-fashioned flavour is dropped by Hemmer Hansen when she translates "med alt det smøre", i.e. "with all that smear"; a Danish equivalent to "asmear" has not been coined, and the English word is not registered by any of the three English-Danish dictionaries.

Clearly, it is easier to talk about equivalence between words from different languages, if we confine ourselves to the denotations of those words; but even so, we have not been very successful in the present study: The normal Danish equivalents to "casualty ward" and "allotment garden" seem to have appeared without any connection to the author who apparently coined the compounds in English. A difficulty may arise in a case like "election cry" in ch.18, p.136: "But I doubt if they had more meaning in them than an election cry." What precisely does that mean? Moltke says "valgråb", a literal translation which is as vague as the English term and, by the way, not recorded by the **ODS**. Hemmer Hansen translates by "valgslogan" (literally "election slogan"), which may be what Dickens had in mind, but the word is not in the **ODS;** our three English-Danish dictionaries do not register "election cry," and once more we cannot find any new coinage in Danish.

Victorian England was in many respects ahead of other nations, e.g. in the field of technology, so names for many new inventions would have to be translated into other languages. Are there any neologisms in **Great Expectations** referring to mechanics and technology? The story is laid in a period when "the steam-traffic on the Thames was far below its present extent" (ch. LIV, p. 413), and Pip goes by coach, not by train; still, we do read about steamers leaving the Pool of London: the steam-age has begun.

We can mention one such neologism, though once more a rather unusual one, viz. "shark-headed screw" or "shark-header", a gross or two of which Joe the blacksmith mentions as a suitable gift to Miss Havisham (ch. 15, p. 104). The **OED** merely informs us that it is "the designation of a kind of screw", but from Nicolas Bentley, Michael Slater and Nina Burgis, **The Dickens Index** (O.U.P., 1988) we learn that shark-headed screws are "round as distinct from flat-headed." Judging from the word's non-appearance in so many dictionaries, even big ones, we may assume that it is not a commonly used term, and not surprisingly it is not found in our three English-Danish dictionaries; Moltke translates it merely by "skruer", i.e. "screws", and apparently the anonymous editor of his translation in the 4th edition (1894) has had his doubts, as he has omitted the mentioning of them; Hemmer Hansen has "skruer med rundt hoved", i.e. "round-headed screws," so no new coinage was made in Danish.

We may add one more Dickensian neologism, a coinage of that age, which appears in **Great Expectations**, but was used by Dickens already in **Sketches by Boz**, ch. VII, "The Steam Excursion", p. 394, viz. "coal-whipper": "..the young ladies exhibited a proper display of horror at the appearance of the coal-whippers and ballast-heavers". Coal-whippers were dockers who raised or "whipped" coal from ships' holds into barges alongside. A rope running over a pulley was attached to a bag of coal in the hold, and the other end was held by the coal-whipper standing on a platform on the deck. As he jumped, the weight of his body weighed the bag of coal, so that it came up from the hold and was deposited into the barge.[2] Coal-whippers worked in gangs, and coal-whipping ceased in the 1880's, when the railways had taken over a considerable share of the transport of coal, and machines had replaced coal-whippers in the ports.[3]

In **Great Expectations**, ch. LIV, p. 413, Dickens gives us a vivid impression of coal-whipping: "..;here, were colliers by the score and score, with the coal-whippers plunging off stages on deck, as counterweights to measures of coal swinging up, which were then rattled over the side into barges." Moltke calls a coal-whipper "kuldrager", which word was preserved by the editor of the 4th edition; in his translation of "The Steam Excursion" he uses the same word, which has, however, in a 1920 edition of the old translation been changed into "kulsjover"; a modern translation of the sketch by Paul Ib Liebe (Charles Dickens, **Skitser og Skildringer** (Copenhagen, 1953), p. 29) has "kullemper", whereas Eva Hemmer Hansen has interpreted Dickens's description as referring to machinery and translates by "taljer", i.e. "pulleys." Clearly, in Moltke's and Liebe's translations no distinction is made between "the coal-whipper", who whipped coal, "the coal-heaver", who unloaded coal from ships by heaving it from one stage to another, and "the coal-backer", who carried the coal on his back. Rosing makes a distinction between the first two terms, translating "coal-heaver" by "kuldrager" and explaining "coal-whipper"; he does not register "coal-backer". Brynildsen lumps all three to-gether, translating by "kul-drager, -sjover". Kjærulff Nielsen has "coal-heaver" translated by "kulafbærer" and "coal-whipper" by "kulhejser", neither of which Danish words is registered by the **ODS**. The other words for are found in that dictionary, "kuldrager" from 1791, "kullemper" from 1883. and "kulsjover" from 1891, so they were not neologisms when they were used by the Dickens translators, and evidently the distinctions between the different groups of workers were not observed in Danish; possibly the method of whipping coal was not used in this country at all.

In some of Dickens's earlier novels there are many more neologisms than in **Great Expectations**, so an examination of their treatment by Danish translators and lexicographers might prove more rewarding than the examination discussed here. Still, a great number of them will be similar to the above examples of words that could scarcely be sources of target-language neologisms. Dickens translations must in many respects have left their mark on the Danish conception of England, have helped to establish the tradition for referring to the country, its products, its institutions etc, but it appears futile to try to describe enrichment of the Danish vocabulary by studying translations of Dickensian neologisms. That would appear to be the main result of the present study, interesting though such an occupation can be in revealing numerous illuminating and frequently amusing details about the vocabularies of the two languages.

NOTES

[1] References to Dickens's work are to the **Oxford illustrated Dickens** edition.

[2] See Charles Dickens: **Great Expectations**. Edited with a critical commentary by G.C.Rosser, M.A. (London, 1964), p. 493.

[3] See R.Newman, "Work and Wages in East London Now and Twenty Years Ago," **The Charity Organisation Review**, No.31, July, 1887 (London), p.275. Coal-whipping is described in great detail in Henry Mayhew, **London Labour and the London Poor**, vol. III (London, 1861), pp. 236-43; copious extracts from that work can be found in **Mayhew's London**, ed. by Peter Quennell (London, 1949), pp. 531-7. The machine that replaced the coal-whippers, the "coal-whipping machine", is described in Edward H,Knight, **The Practical Dictionary of Mechanics**, suppl. (London, 1884), p.206; that must be the "apparatus" which an 1880 example of "coal-whipper" in the **OED** refers to.

Viggo Hjørnager Pedersen

ENGLISH INFLUENCE ON MODERN DANISH VOCABULARY AND ITS IMPLICATIONS FOR DANISH/ENGLISH LEXICOGRAPHY

> ... Licuit semperque licebit
> Signatum præsente nota producere nomen.
> Ut silvae foliis pronos mutantur in annos;
> Prima cadunt: ita verborum vetus interit ætas,
> Et juvenum ritu florent modo nata vigentque.
> Horace: *Ars Poetica*
>
> Poetic licence always must allow,
> As in time past, to modern authors now,
> Leave to present to public use and view
> Words that like coins are stamped with impress new.
> As leaves are changed as gliding years go round,
> Those that bloom first, first strew the forest ground,
> So words grow old and in their course must die,
> While fresh and youthful words their place supply.
> (Transl. Daniel Bagot, 1863)

The following observations originated in my studies of language relativism (i.e. the idea that each language analyses reality in its own way, and that consequently translation is in principle impossible) and are based on my claim that languages in general - and certainly modern Danish - change when foreign language texts are translated into them, and that, in the long run, this facilitates the task of translation.[1]

However, the precise point of the following is slightly different: on the basis of examples, most of which have been culled from material collected for the 3rd ed. of Vinterberg and Bodelsen: **Dansk/Engelsk Ordbog** (hereafter VB3), I want to examine instances of newly developed "translation stock"[2] - constant "equivalents[3]" which are immediately available to the translator and which help to facilitate communication between Danish and English on occasions when a translator encounters certain SL words and phrases for which TL has not so far had any immediate translation.

First, however, let me return to the discussion of language change and whether this is indeed what is happening to Danish at the moment. I shall restate my position and enlarge on some earlier remarks[4], and then discuss new material, viz. selected examples from VB3 and other sources.

Some years ago I wrote an article on the influence on modern Danish of the language approximation now taking place within the EEC (Cf Pedersen (1988: 47-60 and 1989). My main point here was that at the moment languages within the EEC are influencing each other, and that, in particular, major languages like English influence the smaller languages like Danish to such a degree that they come to approach one another, which in its turn means that by degrees it becomes easier to translate from one EEC language into another. To use a paradox: if there is untranslatablity between language A and language B, language B is changed until translation becomes possible.

These views have been criticised by among others Carol Henriksen (1990),[5] who maintains that the examples of change mentioned by me do not document change of the Danish language *system*:

> Even though new words are coming into the Danish language
> due to the influence of the EEC, this does not constitute
> language change. (Henriksen (1990: 16))

This disagreement seems to me to be of general interest, because it raises the question as to what is to be understood by 'language', 'language change', and 'influence', and hence the role of translation in these instances. I do not share the views put forward by Carol Henriksen, and shall go on to explain why.

On Language

Carol Henriksen and I have different views of how the word 'language' is to be understood. From the beginning of this century until very recently, linguistics was dominated by that change of interest which occurred when the predominantly diachronic view of language of the 19th century was replaced by a synchronic one, so that instead of interesting themselves in the word, scholars began to take an interest in the system. This change is illustrated by the fact that whereas Wilhelm von Humboldt (ca. 1820-40) stressed the importance of individual words as conveyors of thought and as problems in connection with translation (because SL and TL can never be completely synonymous) Benjamin Lee Whorf, writing about 100 years later, regarded the language system as much more important than the words, maintaining that languages differ primarily as a consequence of their different systems:

> Sentences, not words, are the essence of speech, just as equations and functions, and not bare numbers, are the real meat of mathematics. We are all mistaken in our common belief that any word (in itself) has an exact meaning. (Whorf 1956: 258; cf. also Pedersen 1988: 40)

However, the fact that a certain view has been common for a long time is no guarantee of its correctness. The interest in comparing languages with mathematics, which is seen in the above Whorf quotation as in so many other linguistic presentations from this century, has indeed led to a number of interesting results, and recently made it possible to study languages by means of computers. But languages are *not* mathematics, and the interest in the language system understood as phonology, morphology, and syntax, has, to a certain extent, diverted attention from what in fact is the most important aspect of language, i.e. that it is a system of signs, meant to further communication and to express and preserve thoughts. If, instead of the mathematical analogy, one were to introduce a biological one, one might say that the grammar of a language is the skeleton and the words the flesh - and then go on to speculate how much milk one could get out of a cow which was nothing but skeleton.

Therefore, I am much more in agreement with Wilhelm von Humboldt than with Whorf, when the former maintains that:

> Die Wörter, und ihre grammatischen Verhältnisse sind zwei in der Vorstellung durchaus verschiedene Dinge. Jene sind die eigentlichen Gegenstände in der Sprache, diese bloss die Verknüpfungen... (Humboldt 1963: 37)

Rejecting the idea that language is an imperfect mathematical model does not mean that one has to reject the idea of all system in language, but the system is less rigid than that of mathematics; it is a system undergoing constant change, and very far from being consistent, unambiguous, or without redundancy. If we return to biology, we might for a moment think of a tree - one which has the right end up and is not standing on its head like the trees of the transformational grammarians. The tree has a definite form with its branches, twigs, and leaves; but this form is not constant: leaves come and go, but also twigs may fall off and be replaced by new ones, and even huge branches may disappear to be replaced by others, giving the tree a very different shape.

It is obvious that a tree which has lost one of its major branches and instead developed more leaves on a couple of the others, is not the same as before. But even if only a single leaf has disappeared, a demonstrable change has still occurred. And if many leaves disappear at the same time, to be replaced by others, the tree is changed, although all the branches are intact. By analogy one might say that the individual loan at word or phrase level is of minimal importance, although it does in fact change the system it forces its way into. But when there is a sudden influx of changes, as is the case in Europe at the moment, something happens to the TL. Furthermore, if the influence is sufficiently long or thorough, the TL is changed in important respects.

The fact that languages change as a consequence of foreign influence is really neither a new nor a controversial assertion. This view is the implicit basis of much traditional criticism of translations as being ungraceful, and as having a bad influence on the TL literature, as e.g. in du Bellay's *Défense et illustration de la langue francaise* (1549) (Cf Pedersen 1987: 18ff).

As in so many other situations, here, too, there is an apt quotation from Dr. Johnson - from the introduction to his *Dictionary* (1755):

> Those who have been persuaded to think well of my design will require that it (viz. the dictionary) should fix our language, and put a stop to those alterations which time and chance have hitherto been suffered to make in it without opposition. With this consequence I confess that I flattered myself for a while; but now begin to fear that I have indulged expectations which neither reason nor experience can justify. When we see men grow old and die at a certain time one after another, from century to century, we laugh at the elixir that promises to prolong life to a thousand years; and with equal justice may the lexicographer be derided, who being able to produce no example of a nation that has preserved their words and phrases from mutability, shall imagine that his dictionary can embalm his language and secure it from corruption and decay, that it is in his power to change sublunary nature, or clear the world at

once from folly, vanity and affectation. ...

Total and sudden transformations of a language seldom happen; conquests and migrations are now very rare: but there are other causes of change, which, though slow in their operation, and invisible in their progress, are perhaps as much superior to human resistance as revolutions of the sky, or intumescence of the tide. Commerce, however necessary, however lucrative, as it depraves the manners, corrupts the language; they that have frequent intercourse with strangers, to whom they endeavour to accomodate themselves, must in time learn a mingled dialect, like the jargon which serves the traffickers on the Mediterranean and Indian coasts. This will not always be confined to the exchange, the warehouse, or the port, but will be communicated by degrees to other ranks of their people, and be at last incorporated with the current speech.

There is another cause of alteration more prevalent than any other, which yet in the present state of the world cannot be obviated. A mixture of two languages will produce a third distinct from both, and they will always be mixed, where the chief part of education and the most conspicuous accomplishment, is skill in ancient or in foreign tongues. He that has long cultivated another language will find its words and combinations crowd upon his memory; and haste and negligence, refinement and affectation will obtrude borrowed terms and exotic expressions.

The great pest of speech is frequency of translation. No book was ever turned from one language into another without imparting something of its native idiom; this is the most mischievous and comprehensive innovation; single words may enter by thousands, and the fabric of the tongue continue the same, but new phraseology changes much at once, it alters not the single stones of the building but the order of the columns. If an academy should be established for the cultivation of our style, which I, who can never wish to see dependence multiplied, hope the spirit of English liberty will hinder or destroy, let them, instead of compiling grammars and dictionaries, endeavour with all their influence to stop the licence of translators, whose idleness and ignorance, if it be suffered to proceed, will reduce us to babble a dialect of France. ...

Asta Steene (1945), Broder Carstensen (1965), Knud Sørensen (1973), and Jørn Lund (1989) are among those who have added to the literature on this subject.

In the following pages I shall not enter into the debate about the influence of English on Danish grammar, even though I maintain that Danish grammar, too, is being subjected to English influence at the moment. Instead, I shall concentrate on individual words, phrases, and idioms, because for closely related languages like Danish and English, it is at these levels especially that difficulties occur, and therefore it is also at this point in particular that approximation between languages is of importance from the point of view of translation theory and strategy.

Annex A shows a number of new words and combinations in VB3 which I find interesting in this connection. The list is taken from the letters **i** and **j**, which constitute roughly 4% of the whole dictionary. There are 83 examples. If this material is representative, this would mean that the whole dictionary contains some 2,000 examples of English loans or Danish neologisms which, without necessarily being borrowed from English, are nevertheless very close to similar English words and constructions; and contrary to the views of Lars Brink in Norman Jørgensen (1991)[6], this is a high figure. For these examples are not to be seen in relation to the total vocabulary of Danish, as does Brink, but only to those parts of it actually in use today, and many of the new loans are of relatively high frequency in modern Danish.

The material may be divided into a number of subcategories:
    1. International (English) abbreviations: IDA, IFC, ILO.
    2. Loans from classical languages which, without actual change (id,

inseminator) or with slight and systematically regular changes are found in both SL and TL, and having virtually the same meaning: Da. idiofon, Eng. idiophone, Da. informatik Eng. informatics, Da. isoperimetrisk, Eng. isoperimetric.

3. Real and tangible loans from material which is not obviously classical or international: in (prep), jazz, job.

4. Calques: idrætsmedicin < sports medicine, ikke-destruktiv < non-destructive, integreret (databehandling) < integrated (data processing), isobarflade < isobaric surface, jordning < earthing.

A hybrid between 3 and 4 consists of words with almost, but not quite, the same form in the two languages: inkonsistent < inconsistent, invers < inverse, ionbalance < ion balance. Many of the words in 2 above belong to this group. However, it is not certain that all the parallels between English and Danish are due to borrowing.

It may indeed be difficult to establish exactly when we have a case of foreign influence. We might agree with Knud Sørensen (1973) that if a TL construction differs from the norm and at the same time resembles an SL construction, it is natural to assume influence.

A parallel list can be extracted from Pia Riber Petersen's *Nye ord i dansk 1955-75*. (Riber Petersen 1984) - cf. Annex B. Although she often refrains from postulating English influence where such influence is likely, but not absolutely proved, nevertheless about 50% of the entries under j are loans from English, or influenced by English; and even in cases where the language of origin for a given word or phrase is doubtful, the parallellism between English and Danish is obvious.

To the lists of individual words which are borrowed from English, or cognate with English words, I have added a list of phrases and collocations taken from the entire collection of slips for VB3, but probably somewhat more influenced by my personal judgment than the list of individual words, because here it is even more difficult to determine whether we have a case of English influence or not. The entire list covers 12 pages, so Annex C lists a selection, giving examples of the different types encountered in my material:

1. Direct loans and loan translations, some of which unmistakably betray their English (or American) origin: *for mange høvdinge og for få indianere, flippe ud*, whereas others are culturally neutral, but happen to have been developed in an English-speaking environment and spread via literature and the media: *med koldt blod, droppe ham som en varm kartoffel*, etc.

2. Parallels; several of these are probably also loans, but they might equally be derived from a common source; see, for example, 2.6, 15, and 22.

2a. A subcategory is made up of those parallels in which our common cultural heritage is clearly seen: The Bible (*den gamle Adam, skille fårene fra bukkene*); the classical tradition (*brød og skuespil, lånte fjer* - from the fable); or folk literature (*Den lille Rødhætte*).

Regarding the whole of category 2 it is worth noting that the parallels imply that at some point or other a translation has taken place - unless we have a case of common Germanic material.

3. A common conceptual basis. This category is less tangible than the preceding ones, but most of the examples here undoubtedly bear witness also to the fact that, at some point or other, a translation has taken place between the languages involved, or from a common source.

Now, what are the implications of these loans for Danish/English lexicography? The traditional attitude - never consistently applied, however - has been to avoid incorporating new loans from English, on the grounds that the translation of such loans is identical with the entry word.

The policy of VB3 has been different. Believing that dictionaries are frequently consulted to check whether, as the user suspects, a given translation is indeed the right one, we want to list all Danish words in common use, together with a good many specialized ones, irrespective of origin. If a translation is in fact identical with the Danish entry, this is indicated by means of a double slanted stroke:

jazz en (mus.) //.

On the other hand, we do advocate, and try to practise, a moderate conservatism. Not all new loans which make the columns of trendy magazines or popular newspapers have come to stay. Ideally, therefore, a word should have been registered and documented in Danish over a period of at least a couple of years, and been found in a number of different sources, before it is admitted to a dictionary. In actual fact, as lexicographers know, one often has to rely on one's intuition when deciding whether to include or reject a word.

It should be emphasized, however, that once a loan has been absorbed by the target language, it takes on a new life there, and may well live on in its new environment, even though it has been lost in the source language.

Butterfly in the sense of 'bow tie', and **sixpence** in the sense of 'cloth cap' were undoubtedly at some point good English colloquialisms; but they have now been lost in these senses in English, whereas they have been preserved in Danish. Likewise the *red thread* which used to be found in all ropes belonging to the British Navy, and could thus be used metaphorically about something unifying, has virtually disappeared from modern English, whereas it is still common in standard Danish.

There is no doubt to me, then, that borrowing is an important cause of language change. To some this seems a shocking idea, to be resisted even at the cost of wilful obtuseness and rejection of reality. I prefer to regard it as a logical consequence of the basic conditions of all life on earth, and a useful reminder that signs do not mean anything in themselves, but only have a meaning for those people who use them for communication. Or in the words of Homer, as interpreted by Alexander Pope, words which, as Horace saw, are no less true about generations of words than of men:

> Like leaves on trees the race of man is found,
> Now green in youth, now withering on the ground;
> Another race the following spring supplies;
> They fall successive, and successive rise;
> So generations in their course decay;
> So flourish these, when those are passed away.

NOTES

[1] Cf. Pedersen (1987: 75 and 1988: 44).

[2] Cf Rabin (1958) and Pedersen (1988: 28f).

[3] The concept of equivalence, made famous in translation theory by E.A Nida (1964) is in fact a somewhat doubtful entity. I shall not go into details here, but merely state my adherence to the view that no two words in two different languages are totally equivalent in all their uses (a Dane may be trekantet, an Englishman square), so that when I use the term, it is simply shorthand for 'the best match I can think of under the circumstances'. For further discussion, cf. Pedersen (1988: 11-29).

[4] Cf. Pedersen (1988: 47-60 and 1991).

[5] See A.L. Jakobsen's review of Pedersen (1988) (Jakobsen 1989) and Carol Henriksen (1989), which is a reaction to the LSP-Newsletter version of an article in Pedersen 1988 (Pedersen 1989), and to the review mentioned above. Carol Henriksen has apparently not read the other articles from Pedersen 1988 where my theoretical views are set forth in more detail, although these articles are referred to in Pedersen (1989).

[6] Quoting Hans Vogt (*Actes*, 6th International Congress of Linguistics, p. 35 (1949), Weinreich (1953: 1) makes the following comment on this issue: "every enrichment or impoverishment of a system involves necessarily the reorganization of all the old distinctive oppositions of the system. To admit that a given element is simply added to the system which receives it without consequences for this system would ruin the very concept of system."

Lyons (1972: 26) has also pronounced on the problem, and especially on the frequently heard but erroneous claim that the so-called 'grammatical words' belong to a class which is immune from change: "We now know that the grammar of a language can also be influenced by that of another language with which it is in contact; and, although ... 'cultural' words are more prone to borrowing than others, it is doubtful whether there is any particular set of words so basic in a language that they are immune from replacement by borrowing.'

BIBLIOGRAPHY

Brink, Lars. "Nordens folkesprog i fare?" in Normann Jørgensen (ed.) *Det danske sprogs status år 2001 - er dansk et truet sprog?* Danmarks Lærerhøjskole, Copenhagen 1991.

Carstensen, B. *Englische Einflüsse auf die deutsche Sprache nach 1945* Heidelberg 1965.

Henriksen, C. "Homeland Danish and the Danish of the EEC Languages out of Contact?" *ALSED-LSP NEWSLETTER* vol 12, 2. Copenhagen 1989.

Jakobsen, A. L. "Tilbage før Babel..." Anmeldelse af *Essays on Translation. Sprint.* 1, 38-44. Copenhagen 1989.

Lund, J. *Okay? amerikansk påvirkning af dansk sprog.* Dansklærerforeningen 1989.

Pedersen, V.H. *Oversættelsesteori.* Copenhagen 1987.

Pedersen, V.H. *Essays on Translation.* Copenhagen 1988.

Pedersen, V.H. "EEC Speak: Some Linguistic Repercussions of the EEC's Languages of Administration, Law and Economics on Modern Danish". *ALSED-LSP Newsletter*, Vol. 11, 2. Copenhagen 1989.

Pedersen, V.H. "Europas sprog som oversættelsesteoretisk problem". To be published in *Terminologie et Traduction 1/1991*, ed. W. Osterheld, European Commission, Luxembourg.

Pia Riber Petersen: *Nye ord i dansk 1955-75.* Copenhagen 1984.

Steene, A. *English Loan-Words in Modern Norwegian.* London 1945.

Sørensen, K. *Engelske lån i dansk.* Copenhagen 1973.

ANNEX A

VB3 I-J

IDA (Den internationale Udviklingssammenslutning)
id (Psykol) //
idémand ideas man
idiofon sb idiophone
idrætsmedicin sports medicine
IFC (Den internationale Finansieringsinstitution)
ikke-destruktiv læsning (edb: non-destructive reading)
ikke-spredningsaftale non proliferation agreement
ikke-voldelig non violent
ILO
image
immersionsdetector immersion detector
immobilisme (polit) immobilism
in (være in)
indefryse (om penge) freeze
indkomstkløft income gap
indeksobligation indexed bond
indhente: han blev -t af sin skæbne fate caught up with him
indkomstloft income ceiling
indre lager edb internal stock, i. storage
industrialisme
industriforskning industrial research
industrisociologi industrial sociology
ineffektiv ineffective
inertinavigationssystem inertial navigation system
infiltrator //
inflation: galoperende i. galloping i.

informant (sprogv) //
informatik informatics
informationsbehandling i. processing
inhalator //
initiativ: det frie i. free enterprise
initiator //
inkonsistent (især mat) inconsistent
innovatør innovator
inoperabel inoperable
inseminator = inseminør, som overs. inseminator
integreret databehandling integrated data processing
intensivafdeling intensive care unit
interessegruppe interest group
interferon (med) //
internalisere (psykol) internalise
interpersonel adj interpersonal (fx. relations)
investeringsbank investment bank (fx den Europæiske I.)
investeringsfond investment fund
invalidevogn invalid car
invers adj inverse
investor //
ionbalance ion balance
isobarflade isobaric surface
isolat (lingv) isolate
isoperimetrisk isoperimetric
jamborette //
jazz //
jazzband j. b.
jazzorkester j. o., j. band
jazztid, -en: the j. age
jetmotor j. m., j. engine

jetpilot j. p.
jihad //
job: springe fra -bet jump the job
jobtryghed j. security
jobløs jobless
jobvurdering j. evaluation
jobtræning j. training
jordning (tlf) earthing
judaisk judaic
juliennesuppe julienne (soup)
jumbo // (fx jet)
jumpsuit j. s.
den juridiske tjeneste (EF) the legal service
juvenilhormon juvenile hormone
jødeharpe Jew's harp

ANNEX B

NYE ORD I DANSK
I - J

I

icebergsalat < iceberg lettuce
idebank
idrætscenter
ikkespredningsaftale
-imperium (fx Hilton-hotelimperiet) "vel efter engelsk empire"
implementere
-in fx teach-in
inddata efter eng. input
inde = in ("det er inde for tiden")
indikator
-indstillet (fx turist-indstillet) efter eng. -minded
industrialist
industrispionage
inflationsrate
influere (begivenhederne)
informatik
informationslcenter, -eksplosion, -teori
informel
ingen kommentar
ingen tvivl om det
initiere
in
input
institutionalisere

instruktor
intensivafdeling
intercitytog
interdisciplinær
interessegruppe
internalisere
interrail
interventionspris
iværksætter efter eng. entrepreneur

j

jackpot
jamme vb
jazzlballet, -rock
jetalder
job (= arbejdsplads)
joblbeskrivelse, - vurdering
joint
joke
jordskredssejr
jukeboks
jumpsuit
-jungle (fx fradrags~)
junk
(-)junta

ANNEX C

PHRASES FROM VB-FILES

1. Loans

1. scorched-earth policy/tactics: den brændte jords politik
2. the abominable snowman: den afskyelige snemand
3. keep a low profile: holde en lav profil
4. loose ends: løse ender
5. sweep the problem under the carpet: feje problemet under (gulv)tæppet
6. get/take/pull one's finger out: få fingeren ud
7. show the flag: vise flaget
8. freak out/flip out: flippe ud
9. galloping inflation: galoperende inflation
10. the man in the street: manden på gaden/gulvet
11. what we lose on the roundabouts we make up on the swings: vi tjener ind på gyngerne hvad vi taber på karussellen.
12. that is his headache: det er hans hovedpine
13. too many chiefs and too few Indians: for mange høvdinge og for få indianere
14. be in: være "in"
15. in cold blood: med koldt blod
16. she is not my cup of tea: hun er ikke min kop te
17. outer space: det ydre rum
18. drop it/him like a hot potato: droppe det/ham som en varm kartoffel
19. free enterprise: det frie initiativ
20. to be caught with one's pants down: at blive taget med bukserne nede
21. to maintain a low profile, at holde en lav profil

2. Parallels

1. free abortion: fri abort

2. lose face: tabe ansigt
3. obey blindly: adlyde blindt
4. the depths of misery: en afgrund af elendighed
5. the evening/twilight of life: livets aften
6. merchants of death: dødens købmænd
7. topical and urgent: aktuel og uopsættelig
8. a share of the cake: en bid/(an)del af kagen
9. attack is the best form of defence: angreb er det bedste forsvar
10. his sweat ran cold on him: han svedte angstens kolde sved
11. he pulled a long face: han blev lang i ansigtet
12. pay under the table: betale under bordet
13. get one's share/slice of the pie: få sin bid af kagen
14. a share of the cake: en bid af kagen
15. he'd bite my head off if...: han ville bide hovedet af mig hvis...
16. boat-shaped neckline: bådformet halsudskæring
17. it's just not me: det er (bare) ikke mig
18. shake like a leaf: ryste som et espeløv
19. his sweat ran cold on him: han svedte angstens kolde sved
20. tight as a clam: tavs som en østers
21. go down the drain: gå i vasken
22. launder black money: vaske sorte penge hvide
23. wrap sby up in cotton wool: pakke én ind i vat og bomuld
24. add fuel to the fire: bære ved til bålet
25. (a fate) worse than death: det, der er værre end døden

2a. Common Cultural Background

1. the old Adam came out in him: den gamle Adam kom op i ham
2. man is made in the image and likeness of God: mennesket er Guds afbillede
3. the pit of iniquity: lastens/syndens afgrund
4. the depths/recesses of the human soul: sjælens dybeste afgrund

5. separate the sheep from the goats: skille fårene fra bukkene
6. throw the baby out with the bath water: kaste barnet ud med **badevandet**
7. bread and circuses: brød og skuespil
8. borrowed feathers: lånte fjer
9. get off the high horse: komme ned fra den høje hest
10. an iron hand in a velvet glove: en jernhånd i en fløjlshandske
11. it was a night of long knives: det var de lange knives nat
12. a colossus with feet of clay: en kolos på lerfødder
13. bear one's cross: bære sit kors
14. the forces of darkness: mørkets magter
15. Little Red Ridinghood: Den lille Rødhætte
16. take (it) with a grain of salt: tage noget med et korn/gran **salt**

3. Common Conceptual Basis
1. freak out/go ape/go bananas: gå agurk
2. bend/lift the elbow: bøje armen
3. have to pinch oneself: måtte knibe sig i armen
4. knock on wood: banke (3 gange) under bordet
5. get out of bed on the wrong side: få det forkerte ben først ud **af sengen**
6. purple with rage: blå/kobberrød i ansigtet af vrede
7. cut the bough one stands upon: save den gren over man selv **sidder på**
8. fed up to the (back) teeth: hænge én langt ud af halsen
9. stir up a hornets' nest: stikke hånden i en hvepserede
10. drunk as a fish: fuld som en pave
11. still wet behind the ears: endnu ikke tør bag ørene
12. pounds and pence: kroner og øre
13. sit (etc) with a face like thunder: ligne en tordensky
14. get back to the grindstone: komme tilbage til trædemøllen

Jørgen Harrit

POSSESSION AND EXISTENCE

A Problem in Active Danish-Russian Lexicography

The most important challenge - and at the same time that which is most difficult to tackle - to an active Danish-Russian dictionary consists in leading the user safely to the correct translation of a given Danish text into Russian. I deliberately use the word 'the correct translation', because my experience within the field of Danish-Russian translation tells me that in non-fiction it is in principle always, and in fiction in most cases possible to point to one and only one translation as the best. With the proviso that the individual translator's subjective preference for one of two or more absolute synonyms such as Danish *skelne* and *sondre* may lead to divergencies of a purely verbal nature in the final form of the translation.

If these challenges are to be met, the lexicographer himself must understand and then work up the linguistic essence of the problems in a number of central fields where source and target language differ, such as in the syntactico-semantical field, in such a way that it may be described in a form which is adequate for the user of the dictionary, as well for the use of the dictionary. The difficulties are many and varied, and of course there are great differences between individual pairs of languages. There are undoubtedly different problems in preparing e.g. a Danish-Swedish and a Danish-Russian dictionary. In the following, I shall demonstrate one such problem which proves to be rather complex, as is always the case, but which leads to some interesting results.

Existential- or BE-clauses, i.e. clauses which basically express some form of the existence or being of the subject, are probably known in all languages, but they only become lexicographically relevant at the moment when they are differently expressed in the source and target language. Concerning Danish-Russian, the problem is particularly acute in connection with the negation of existence. Therefore we have to begin with a few words about this area.

Negation. In Danish negation of a sentence is a simple matter in that we just insert the negation *ikke* after the finite verb. There are many differences between Danish and Russian, but the most important one is that in Be-clauses Russian uses the specific particle of negation не (in the preterite and the future however нет было and не будет respectively) and at the same time takes the subject in the genitive. As according to the case theory of Roman Jakobson[1] the genitive is a case of extent, this means that any limitation of the category of existence has the same linguistic impact. Below follow the relevant parts of the article *ikke* in the Danish-Russian dictionary:

> **ikke** *adv* **A** *(generel negation)* не ☐ *han kommer* ~ он не придёт ; *hvis han ~ kommer, (så) kommer jeg heller ~* если он не придёт, (то) я тоже не приду; *jeg håber ~, (at) vi kommer for sent* я надеюсь, что мы не опоздаем ; *han sagde ~ mere* он больше ничего не сказал
>
> **B** *(partiel negation)* не ☐ *det var ~ mig men ham, der gjorde det* это сделал не я, а он; *det var ham og ~ mig, der gjorde det* это сделал он, а не я

C *(eksistensnegation)* **a** нет‧‧нé было‧‧не бу́дет ◻ *han er ~ hjemme* его́ нет до́ма **b** *(med visse andre vb, som kan udtrykke eksistens, f.eks.:) der findes ~ et sådant menneske* не существу́ет тако́го челове́ка **c** *~ en, ~ et, ~ nogen, ~ noget, ingen, intet*

This head is followed by a foot with detailed illustrations of usage.

This excerpt demonstrates a well-known paradox. Although Danish is the source language so that it is the Danish entry *ikke* which is the starting point of the description, the structure of the article is entirely decided by features of Russian. The subdivision into the headings general (A), partial (B), and existential (C) negation is irrelevant for Danish, but made necessary because the negating particle in Russian is placed differently in (A) and (B), whereas in (C) it differs radically from (A) and (B). Finally, under C.c there is a reference to the articles *ingen* and *intet*. The importance of this will appear from the below.

Possession is mostly expressed in Danish by the verb *have*, a.o. Russian likewise has several ways of expressing possession, but the relevant ones in this connection are the verb (1) име́ть 'to have' with the accusative object and the model such as (2): у меня́ есть маши́на 'I have a car'. The dictionary entry for *have* must first be able to explain when (1) and (2) are used. (1) is most often seen with an abstract object, and in certain idioms such as:

(3) я име́ю честь   'I have the honour (to)'

Here

(4) у меня́ есть честь

would mean 'I am a man of honour' and thus be clearly differentiated from (3). The phrase:

(5) я име́ю маши́ну   'I have a car'

is rejected by ordinary usage, although it is correct from the point of view of the language system. Thus to distinguish between (1) and (2), the features [+abstract object] and [+idiom] are used.

Possession and Existence. (2) is the perfect equivalent of the Danish 'I have a car', but really the words mean 'with me there is (= exists) a car'. (2) in other words is a Be-clause with the syntactic structure [adverbial of place + finite 'be' + subject]. Let us look more closely at the Russian variations on the theme 'to have a car':

(2) у меня́ есть маши́на   'I have a car'
(6) у меня́ но́вая маши́на   'I have a new car'
(7) у меня́ маши́на (, а у тебя́ мопе́д)   'I have (a) car
                                    (, and you have (a) moped')
(8) у меня́ е́сть но́вая маши́на   'I have a new car'

In (6) and (7) the finite verb is formally lacking, i.e. it appears in a zero form, which is normal in Russian Be-clauses in the present tense. In (8) the verb of existence would normally be accentuated, i.e. existence would be underlined. The dictionary has to make explicit the difference in use between (2) and (7), and (6) and (8). This happens partly by an **NB!**-instruction peculiar to this dictionary (see below), and partly by the use of examples in the foot of the article.

The negation of possession looks as follows, when we concentrate on (2) with its variations:

(9) у меня нет машины 'I do not have a car/I have no car'
(10) у меня ненóвая (= стáрая) машина 'I have a non-new (= old) car'
(11) у меня не машина (, а мопéд) 'I do not have a car (, but a moped)'
(12) у меня нéт нóвой машины 'I do not have a new car/ I have no new car'

If these interpretations are correct, only (9) and (12) are examples of a general negation of existence (of (2) and (8) respectively). (11) seems to be a partial negation of a characterization. Furthermore, (7) seems to be the positive contrast to the partial negation in (11), and (6) to combine existence with characterization which is why (6) may be paraphrased as 'I have a car, and it is new' and (7) 'what I have is a car'.

The Concept of Antonomy is manifested grammatically in the correlation 'positive/negative' and lexically in the correlation 'new/old'. We shall now see how this concept is the only tool which makes it possible to identify and handle a very important type of Russian Have-clauses. In the excerpt from the article *ikke* there was a reference to the articles *ingen* and *intet* under C.c. This is because Russian has two negative pronouns нéкого 'there is nobody who' and нéчего 'there is nothing which' together with the negative adverbs нéгде 'there is no place where', нéкуда 'there is no place whither', нéоткуда 'there is no place from where' and нéкогда 'there is no time to'. They all express negative existence. A couple of examples:

(13) нé с кем говори́ть 'there is nobody to talk to'

(14) не́ с кем бы́ло мне говори́ть	'there was nobody for me to talk to = I had nobody to talk to'
(15) не́где спать	'there is no place to sleep'
(16) мне не́где спать	'I have no place to sleep'

The **antonyms** look as follows:

(17) есть с кем говори́ть	'there is somebody to talk to'
(18) мне бы́ло с кем говори́ть	'I had somebody to talk to'
(19) есть где спать	'there is a place to sleep'
(20) мне есть где спать	'I have a place to sleep'

Conclusion : Consequently the dictionary entry for *have* must introduce and handle the items есть кто, есть что, есть где, есть куда, есть откуда and есть когда as the positive versions of the above negative pronouns and adverbs. To my knowledge this has never been done in any bilingual dictionary into Russian – or for that matter in any monolingual dictionary of Russian.

Apart from the differences in meaning, expressions of types (2) and (13/14) with variations furthermore demonstrate clear differences as to syntactic structure, which makes it even more necessary to describe them in the dictionary. However, this may easily lead us into the interesting discussion as to the place and importance of grammar for dictionaries, which is not what I want in this paper, as I have only wanted to give an example of a concrete analysis in connection with the redaction of one out of many complicated articles in an active Danish-Russian dictionary describing i.a. grammatical words. Below follow the relevant sections of the article *have:*

have *vb* име́ть *(især med abstrakt obj. og i faste vendinger); (besidde som ejendom også)* владе́ть *(+I); (besidde, være ihændehaver af også)* облада́ть *(+I)*

NB! *Oftest bruges modellen:* у +G {есть •• был •• бу́дет} +N, *f.eks.: jeg har en bil* у меня́ есть маши́на. *Med negation:* у +G {нет •• не́ было •• не бу́дет} маши́ны ; *i visse tilfælde kan vb udelades, f.eks.: jeg har (en) bil, og du har (en) knallert* у меня́ маши́на, а у тебя́ мопе́д

NB! *antonymerne til* не́кого, не́чего, не́где, не́куда, не́откуда, не́когда *hhv.* есть кто, есть что, есть где, есть куда, есть откуда, есть когда, *f.eks.: jeg hár nogen at tale med* мне есть с кем (по)говори́ть; *jeg hávde et sted at sove* мне бы́ло где спать; (⇔ *ikke, ingen, intet)*

PS After the signs ☐ and ■ in this case there are two separate feet with detailed illustrations of usage. The notation differs from that of other bilingual dictionaries a.o. because comma and semicolon must have unambiguous functions. In this dictionary comma is only used in its syntactic function, whereas semicolon separates meanings in the head of the article and examples of usage in its foot. Synonymous translation equivalents are separated with a raised dot (•), partially synonymous equivalents by a raised double dot (••) and the sign separates various examples og usage by telescoping. The signs { and } indicate the beginning and the end of a case of telescoping respectively. The signs → ⇔ mean: see and see also respectively.

(1) Roman Jakobson, *Beitrag zur allgemeinen Kasuslehre: "Gesamtbedeutungen der russischen Kasus"* (TCLP, VI, 1936) in: "Selected Writings", vol. II, Mouton, The Hague, 1971.

Ellen M. Pedersen

SYNONYMICS AFTER CHOMSKY: A CHALLENGE IN PROGRESS

I

To lexicographers educated into Chomskyan linguistics, every language consists of an infinite set of sentences. The syntactic conception of grammar that ensues makes in-depth analysis of each language necessary but, because levels become incomparable, hampers word-to-word analysis across language lines.

Since contrastive analysis is part and parcel of lexicography (as of translation), the compilers of a new Danish-English Synonymics Base have had to adapt their conceptual structure to the task at hand. The methods used for the initial phase were suitably complementary.

The compilers have had to admit to one initial, negative assumption: Post-Chomskyan linguists have lived through linguistically and ethically complex times. We can no longer believe in classical, simple-minded definitions of the synonym. This means that although it it possible to learn from our predecessors we have had to redefine the synonym. Our definition is offered internationally for discussion here for the first time.

II

Danish users of a Danish-English dictionary or base typically ask, 'What is this in English?' They assume, in other words, that native speakers of both languages feel the same phenomenon to exist, to be real. They assume it to be kept distinct from other phenomena in identical or at least similar ways. More basically and controversially (we would like to remind fellow professionals), they assume the same truths to abide in both languages. The distinction between the bipartite units of true vs. false and real vs. unreal is blurred in everyday language (cf. the amplificative, booster usage 'a real gentleman', 'a real s.o.b'). In offering a dictionary, a word-book, rather than a sentence-book, we therefore, in agreement with users of everyday language, skip the unit of true vs. false. Instead, we assume that the user of the base under development intends, in deliberate and polished, written English, to state what the user holds true, and offer a selection of single words to pick as tools.

As the Danish philologist Lisbeth Falster Jakobsen has pointed out, the signs used to evoke a certain content depend on how much instruction one feels is the receiver's due.[1] Identical states of affairs, *Sachverhalte*, may be conceptualised in several different ways. So, principles of lexation differ monolingually from situation to situation, and vary with communicational needs. Danish and English, too, uphold overall principles that are different, at times radically so. 'Natural' examples appear in journalism: when an American dancer tells a Danish journalist 'I have learned...', a thoughtless journalist may translate her confidence, '*Jeg har lært*'. Such word-by-word transmission to Danish readers will indicate that the dancer is fresh out of class with rotes intact, whereas what the dancer means to imply in original Danish is more likely to read, '*Det er min erfaring*', 'It is my [collected, preserved and available] experience]', cf. *Collins English*'s 'accumulated knowledge'.

Too, on single element level, Danish and English present interesting degrees of incompatibility. Translators into Danish repeatedly have to replace 'there' with 'here', or with nothing, 'this' with 'that', 'go' with 'come'; and, once a target sentence has been framed, definite and indefinite elements, articles in particular, have been known to swap positions. The first two sets indicate a different deictic sensibility; the third is part of the English subset, unique in its completeness, including I-you, this-that, here-there, come-go, and bring-take; the fourth set reflects, besides different notions of familiarity among readers with different linguistic backgrounds, the different status of the definite article: the Danish definite article actively defines, whereas in English the article is merely elective, requiring further epexegesis, elaborative paraphrase, or simply explanation.

Both languages share the problem, more keenly felt with certain word classes than with others, which R.H. Robbins has described as the 'fuzzy borders' of semantic features.

> We can and do create all manner of artifacts in all sorts of feature gradations. The point is that [whereas] phonological features belong to the finite resources with which language operates... semantic features attempt to bring some order, and succeed only to a limited extent, into the infinite use that we make of these resources in meaningful discourse about the world we share...

To which Robbins added, quoting Kempson's understatement, relevant to philosophy as well as linguistics, 'The theoretical status of semantic components is highly problematical.'[2]

The compilers of this base will only importune users with problems on this level if actual new developments are involved, but we have had to remain generally aware of them. Different principles of conceptualisation are directly reflected in the completed portion, however, as is the incompatibility described above.

III

Members of the compilers' generation of linguists have had understandable reservations about the project. 'The synonym does not exist,' was the standard reaction. True, as I said above, the synonym does not exist in the classical, simple-minded sense of 'word identical & coextensive in sense & usage with another of the same language' etc, nor, as to Peter Erasmus Müller, creator of the Danish classic, *Dansk Synonymik eller Forklaring af eenstydige danske Ord* (1829), [Explanation of monoreferential Danish words], *eenstydig*, implying one reference, one sense, or one meaning per entry.[3]

Since the present project exists even if the synonym as such is part of an outdated belief system, the compilers, working alternately from positive and negative assumptions, have produced a tentative definition. As in all the humanities, what matters initially is where the argument begins. We begin by asking, What is idiomatic language? By idiomatic we mean 1) what is right rather than wrong, and 2) what is contemporary rather than outdated. 2) is most interesting and challenging. Two examples may serve to illustrate the rashness of fast answers, telling us that a secondary condition may be necessary, namely, What can the receiver be expected to perceive, remember, or accept? The first example is known to creative users of the written language: it is possible to enrich a description or a statement by using an outdated or quaint adjective, reviving it, as it were. The second example was a find: a group of Aarhus scholars in a Danish article contrast the use of German and Danish verbs, saying, *I reglen arbejder vi med tilfælde, hvor eet ord i det danske svarer til flere ord i det tyske* [We are concerned with, as a rule, the type of case where one Danish word may replace more than a single German one].[4] '*I det danske... tyske...*', *'in the Danish... German...' they tell us. Now, 'in the German' was standard Danish in Müller's days. Having been generally replaced with *på tysk,* *'on German' it seemed to have disappeared, and I was planning to do an informal questionaire, meaning to test contemporary tolerance vis-à-vis the expression. Obviously, it was possible for those colleagues to revive it and feel they were making themselves understood to their target audience: teachers of German.

It is possible to start actual definitorial proceedings in two ways, a positive, and a more fruitful negative one. The positive strategy involves seeking idiomatic expressions in the sense of chains of words, neither of which is replaceable, expressions whose 'meaning' goes beyond the meaning of the sum of the words. Is is possible, further, to order these expressions by type, 'go west' in English, for example, representing one type, 'kick the bucket' another (or, to content-oriented compilers, the same) 'buy a pig in a poke' a third which, incidentally, in Danish is *the* cat in *the* sack, 'take the bull by the horns' a fourth, 'talk turkey' a fifth. Such ready-made expressions give access to an epistemological level shared by groups of languages, and are interesting in a pre-linguistic sort of way. A recent Danish effort has shown similarities between Danish, English, German, and French expressions, similarities that remind us of the body, cf. *tage én ved næsen*, 'take somebody by the nose', of work and its products, cf. 'hit the nail on the head', and of the agrarian base that we share in spite of different degrees and types of industrialisation, cf. the 'bull' mentioned above, which exists in all four languages.

The second, negative strategy begins with a search for difference rather than sameness: those elements are idiomatic which need changing as soon as we try to render their meaning in another language, 'go' in a specific context rather than 'come', for example. Working from this strategy, we find the dynamics of each language, its principles of idiomatisation. On this level, languages live and grow. Synonymics, the study of signs and their content, becomes the study of the single words whose combinations affirm, maintain, and continue the idiomatic process unique to the language. The synonym is the linguistic unit with which we build, preserve, and innovate idiomatic Danish, English, etc.

This definition does not exclude metonymic phrases like the ones mentioned above; the single word is allowed its right to combine, attract, and reject. By assuming the adjective 'idiomatic' we avoid definitorial hermeticism, and in using the verbal noun 'idiomatisation' (from Wallace

Chafe) we take into account the different intensity and speed of these processes - an expression made up of a string of completely irreplaceable elements is under slow idiomatisation and, particularly, de-idiomatisation: how many generations of city-dwellers does it take to forget the bull's horns or the pig in the poke?

IV

Definitorial manoeuvres notwithstanding, we have been able to learn from previous achievements; from Peter Erasmus Müller, and later Harry Andersen, how the world is seen in Danish terms; from Peter Roget how to organise concepts in a word-book; and from Henning Næsted, whose 1946 dictionary *Engelsk-Dansk Synonym-Ordbog* is our antecedent, how 'synonyms' were organised two generations ago. Peter Erasmus is felt to be old because, although edited and ordered by somebody else, his work was not updated unlike that of Peter Roget, who inspired him as he inspired everybody else working with 'synonymics' in this *kulturkreis*. Henning Næsted's *Engelsk-Dansk Synonym-Ordbog* (whose title belies its direction) was published before Vinterberg & Bodelsen's *Dansk Engelsk Ordbog*, the largest of its kind, a fact which is obvious from Næsted's assumptions and explanations. Working with synonymics today, we are able to assume, without taking recourse to direct reference, user familiarity with conventional word-to-word dictionaries. Unlike Roget's and later monolingual thesauri, the present venture cannot only be a list. It is a thesaurus-type base whose entry words are Danish. We can argue, and after fifty years without a book of this kind we must.

V

We hear the voices of the innocent: how does one render the epitomal Danish adjective *hyggelig*? We are prepared to advise users in common language terms that in meaning to describe a locality and a mood, perhaps they want a sentence with a different structure than <noun> <verb>

hyggelig. 'The place had atmosphere' is an option taken from one of our sources. In a more dangerous area, the innocent may ask, Doesn't the noun 'experience' come in two parts? Contrastively and roughly it does, Danish having the 'equivalent' of *Erlebnis* versus *Erfahrung*, a well-known problem in translations into English of non Anglo-Germanic philosophy. The compilers are not innocent on this point, being familiar with John Dewey's attempt to settle the issue (against both Locke and Hume) in which he, modestly compared with several popular monolingual dictionaries, adduces *four* types of experience. Here, again, it must be possible to discuss how users will most precisely and satisfactorily provide the information needed, whether by a single word or a string of words. As professional translators know, the single word asserts itself in a number of ways but is not sacred.

Users who are willing to abstract from word-by-word contrastive analysis get an estimate of 5000 entries with partly authentic examples. To readers of versatile target language material, finding authentic examples requires a different reader strategy, a change of perspective from literary, critical, etc., but is not difficult.

We assume more than a willingness to learn to show the way to The Little Mermaid (and will have to, having already assumed that our users want to *write*). And suggest, for user's aims, the following, rather conventional, five points:

1) To approximate as closely as possible what the user wants to say; what we had above as 'to state what the user holds true'
2) To find the word evoking as many desirable, and as few undesirable, connotations a possible
3) To avoid the repetitiousness stemming from lexical poverty or from the slower mental leafing typical of (even very advanced) second language learners

4) To enrich the user's English with a flexible choice of words that the user may not approach as problems ('big' will often be adequate but English without 'large', 'huge', 'vast' etc., becomes stereotype
5) To avoid, to some degree, 'mistakes' stemming from the idea that homographical elements in the two languages are the same 'word.' 'To some degree' only, because we assume *a priori* knowledge that they are not. One counter-example, a familiar trap, taken from a recent translation into Danish: *genial*, 'ingenious', 'brilliant', used for 'genial', *imødekommende* etc., whose coverage is not even vaguely similar.

What about the questions that users do not ask because the 'equivalent' of something in English is zero in Danish? A user suspecting something like the subsystem of come-go and bring-take will make a random guess at where we have put it, or not suspect that it is there at all. A user needing an overview of the special problems connected with 'sexist' language in English, and current attempts to solve them, is equally lost. In order to cover these and similar lexico-technical issues, we have introduced, not a separate class of front matter, which we find offputting, but thematic entries with ad hoc headwords, and an additional list of these thematic entries, much in the manner of an encyclopedia. In this way it is possible, furthermore, to cover general issues such as current developments involving word-classes, semantic sliding, etc. unique to English.

Funding beyond the 30 pages of base and 60 pages of theory already completed is under negotiation. The plan is to continue working on macro-level, recording all data electronically. Future editors will be able to publish small or large portions in book form.

NOTES

[1] "Ekvivalens i kontrastiv lingvistik". *Oversættelseskredsen* (Copenhagen lectures on translation and lexicgraphy organised by Cay Dollerup), 27 March 1990.

[2] Burchfield, Robert (ed.). *Studies in Lexicography*. Oxford: Clarendon 1987: 63.

[3] Peter Erasmus Müller (1776-1834), who ended his career as bishop of Zealand, became the first Danish historiographer and is known chiefly as a scholar of Icelandic literature. He failed to complete the philological side of his studies, but with his synomymics published one of the most significant works on standard Danish before 1860.

[4] Per Bærentzen. "Tyske synonymer set fra dansk, eksemplificeret ved *true: drohen/bedrohen*". Erik Andersen & Gunnar Frost Olesen (eds.). *Forskning i fremmedsprogspædagogik*. Arkona 1979: 194 (Statens Humanistiske Forskningsråds Symposium 1978).

The author wishes to thank Dorte Albrechtsen for looking once again for a missing reference.

Arne Zettersten

TOOLS FOR THE HISTORICAL LINGUIST:
Innovations in the use of English historical dictionaries, corpora and databases.

During the past 10-15 years, the historical linguist has been fortunate enough to find extremely powerful and useful new tools at his disposal in the form of new computerized dictionaries, linguistic corpora, concordances, text archives, databases, and other computer-based knowledge banks. In addition to such collections of data, the electronic revolution has brought about a number of new storage and retrieval techniques, which add a totally new dimension to the existing data. New media such as CD-ROM, videodiscs, and online databases have further increased the possibility of distributing and exchanging linguistic data.

English language scholars have had the particular advantage of access to more historical dictionaries, more tools and more data than colleagues working on other languages. The purpose of the present paper is to discuss the current status of historical English dictionaries, corpora and databases and the special ways of retrieving information from such collections of data. My view is that the use of collections of historical data has become much more dynamic and effective thanks to the emergence of new media, new techniques, and new projects concerned with historical lexicography.

The Oxford English Dictionary (OED)
The *New* or *Oxford English Dictionary (OED)*, published in 1933, has since then been considered the central source of information on the English wordstock by most scholars. The four-volume *Supplement to the Oxford English Dictionary* (edited by R.W. Burchfield in 1972-86) provided a most important addition to the original dictionary. A further step was taken in

1984, when the *New Oxford English Dictionary* Project launched the first phase of an extensive plan to produce a printed integrated *OED* as well as an electronic database.

The printed integrated edition of the original *OED* with the *Supplements* was published in 20 volumes by Oxford University Press in 1989. The project work on the integrated dictionary and the database was based on the cooperation between Oxford University Press, International Computaprint Corporation (ICC), Fort Washington, U.S., IBM United Kingdom Ltd., and the University of Waterloo, Canada.[1]

All the material of *OED* and the Supplements were keyboarded by more than a hundred typists at ICC, before the prof-reading, the mark-up procedure and the parsing work started.

The second phase of the *New OED* Project dealt with the establishment of an electronic version, a database which will be able to answer all kinds of lexical inquiries. One of the main advantages of this database is that the dictionary can be constantly revised and updated. Another advantage is the great potential of future spin-off dictionaries, e.g. dictionaries for regional varieties or dictionaries of English for special purposes. It has even been suggested[2] that a composite world dictionary of all national and regional varieties of English, leaving out a common core, could be produced.

Further advantages for scholars are the excellent possibilities of access to specific information on all kinds of linguistic, literary or cultural problems that can be retrieved from the database. Finally, the database is commercially available in online format as well as CD-ROM format. The first CD-ROM version of *OED* without the supplements was published in 1989[3] by Oxford University Press in collaboration with Tri Star Publishing.

The period dictionaries
It is clear to most of us now that the *New OED* can be the basis for a variety of new wordlists and dictionaries. It was also quite clear to W.A. Craigie back in 1919 that the original material of the original *OED* could be the basis for a series of so-called period dictionaries. In a paper delivered in 1919 at the Philological Society in London, 'New Dictionary Schemes', Craigie launched his proposal for a series of separate historical dictionaries which could have access to the stock of *OED*'s quotation slips for the periods in question.

Craigie's scheme reproduced below is based on a diagram printed by A.J. Aitken (1987)[4] who in his turn adapted it from one first published by C.C. Fries in 1932.[5]

Table 1

The Dictionary of Old English (DOE)
In 1969, the Centre for Medieval Studies of the University of Toronto launched its plan to sponsor a new *Dictionary of Old English (DOE)*, edited by Angus Cameron and C.J.E. Ball. The whole corpus of Old English material covering c. 3 million words was converted to machine-readable form by 1979. In 1980, *A Microfiche Concordance to Old English (PDOE 1)* and *The List of Texts and Index of Editions* appeared, followed in 1985 by *A Michrofiche Concordance to Old English: The High Frequency Words (PDOE 2)*. The two computer-made concordances (1980 and 1985) provide the contexts of each word-token in the entire corpus of Old English, a very valuable research tool for Anglo-Saxon scholars.

The first part of the *Dictionary of Old English* on microfiche (fascicle D) appeared in 1986.[6]

The Middle English Dictionary (MED)
The *Middle English Dictionary (MED)* took over about 430,000 quotations from *OED* as from the start of its planning period in 1925. The first part of the dictionary appeared in 1952 edited by Hans Kurath and Sherman M. Kuhn and it has now reached the end of the letter *S*.[7] The total number of pages of the complete dictionary will probably be c. 14,000 pages with nearly a total of 800,000 examples. The total number of main entries will be more than 45,000. *MED* does not exist in computerized form but a new computer-assisted system for producing camera-ready copy has been introduced.[8]

The Early Modern English Dictionary (EMED)
The work on the *Early Modern English Dictionary* started in 1927 under the leadership of C.C. Fries at the University of Michigan, taking over c. 2 1/2 millions of *OED* quotations from Early Modern English. A very extensive excerption programme was initiated by Fries, involving as many

as 460 excerptors and eight assistants. Due to lack of resources the work on *EMED* had to close down in 1939.

The interest in *EMED* was revived by R.C. Alston at Leeds in 1965 and later at the University of Michigan, Ann Arbor, by Richard Bailey and Jay L. Robinson. In 1975, Bailey and Robinson, together with J.B. Downer, published a portion of the *EMED* collection in microfiche form in *Michigan Early Modern English Materials* (*MEMEM*). It was quite clear that the amount of work and the costs for making a full *EMED* were too prohibitive at that time, even though the microfiche technique is an ideal way of saving space and costs. Is seems that *EMED* will have to wait for the full publication of *MED* and the future additions to the *New OED* database. It was suggested by Jürgen Schäfer[9] that scholars all over the world should contribute to a joint database serving both the *New OED* and *EMED*.

The Scottish dictionaries

A Dictionary of the Older Scottish Tongue (*DOST*) was started by W.A. Craigie before he presented his scheme of period dictionaries in 1919.[10] In 1964 A.J. Aitken, the Chief Editor, and Paul Bratley created the Older Scottish Textual Archive of computer-readable Older Scots Texts at the University of Edinburgh, consisting of c. 1 million words of running text. This has been the basis of a concordance for the use of the dictionary work and also for separate linguistic analyses.[11]

The *Scottish National Dictionary* (*SND*) was launched in 1929 and the final volume (out of ten) was published in 1976 under the editorship of David D. Murison. In 1954 the dictionary was moved from Aberdeen to Edinburgh.

The American period dictionaries

A Dictionary of American English on Historical Principles (*DAE*) was published in 1944 by Chicago University Press in twenty parts (4 vols.). The dictionary was edited by W.A. Craigie and J.R. Hulbert. There is also a dictionary, based on *DAE*, called *A Dictionary of Americanisms on Historical Principles* (*DA*), edited in 1951 by Mitford M. Mathews. This two-volume dictionary was composed of words that originated in the U.S.

Regional dictionaries

Of all the regional dictionaries the *Dictionary of American Regional English* (*DARE*) is the most extensive one. Further, the dictionary project has been pioneering in two ways: it was first in basing a historical dictionary on both spoken and written sources and it began to make use of computers as early as 1965.[12] The first volume (out of five), edited by Frederic G. Cassidy, appeared in 1985. As pointed out by Cassidy,[13] "every computer aid that seems affordable is being applied". Particularly the mapping procedure is very impressive, the number of maps in vol. I being over 550.[14]

In addition to his work as Chief Editor of *DARE*, Frederic G. Cassidy was a pioneer in being an editor (together with R.B. Le Page) of the first of several dictionaries of 'new Englishes', namely the *Dictionary of Jamaican English* (*DJE*), which appeared in 1967 (2nd ed. 1980). In the same year, *A Dictionary of Canadianisms on Historical Principles* (*DC*) also appeared, edited by W.S. Avis. A number of dictionaries illustrating the rich variability of English have since appeared, most of them being important additions to this branch of historical lexicography. Other dictionaries, like *DJE* and *DC*, follow the pattern of *OED*. This is true of the *Dictionary of Newfoundland English* (*DNE*) and of the *Dictionary of Bahamian English* (*DBE*), and of the *Australian National Dictionary* (*AND*), edited by W.S. Ramson (1988). These and some other recent dictionaries, like *A Dictionary of South African English on Historical Principles* (*DSAE*), ed. by J. Branford in 1989, and the *Dictionary of Caribbean English and Usage*

(*DCEU*), by R. Allsopp, may be called 'dictionaries of translated varieties of English'.[15] On the question of dictionaries of English-related pidgins and creoles, see Görlach, M., 'Lexicographical Problems of New Englishes and English-related Pidgin and Creole Languages', *English World-Wide*, 6 (1985), 1-36.

Dialect dictionaries

The *English Dialect Dictionary* (*EDD*) by Joseph Wright, published in 1898-1905, has for a long time been the standard source of information for English dialectologists. All the linguistic atlases, which have since then been published on both sides of the Atlantic, have provided an enormous amount of new data. As pointed out above, the information from American atlases has been carefully made use of for the work on *DARE*.

Nowadays, both the English Dialect Society and the American Dialect Society make use of computers in various ways, for example for mapping programs.

In the recent *A Linguistic Atlas of Late Mediaeval English* (1986) by Angus McIntosh, M.L. Samuels and Michael Benskin, all the item maps and dot maps were produced by computer programs and printed by a phototypesetter.

One example of the computerization of dialect data is Wolfgang Viereck's project at the University of Bamberg, based on the lexical, morphological and syntactic material of the *Survey of English Dialects* at Leeds.[16] Another example is the Helsinki Corpus of English Texts. One part of this historical corpus is a corpus of present-day British English dialects. Ossi Ihalainen, the leader of this part of the project, has shown among other things that a tool like the dBase III data management system can be used to retrieve and organise linguistic information successfully.[17] Similarly, Louis Janus and Greg Shadduck have indicated some flexible alternative procedures for analysing texts by using the dBase III and another general purpose software package, Lotus 1-2-3.[18]

Slang dictionaries and dictionaries of new words

The leading dictionaries of slang are Eric Partridge's *A Dictionary of Slang and Unconventional English* (8th ed. 1984) and Wentworth-Flexner's *Dictionary of American Slang* (2nd ed. 1975), revised and updated by R.L. Chapman in 1986 and renamed *New Dictionary of American Slang*. In addition to these, there are numerous slang dictionaries on the market. Generally, slang dictionaries have been regarded as containing rather poor information on etymology. With the emergence of databases like the *New OED* database, a limited but new way of retrieving information on dialect words and slang can be utilized.

New words in the English language are continuously presented in the Barnhart Dictionaries and Quarterly Companions and in articles by J. Algeo - A. Algeo in *American Speech*. See also J. Ayto, *The Longman Register of New Words* (1989). H.M. Logan has made an interesting study of the ways in which new words are created in English at various periods by analysing the *New OED* database by PAT, the inquiry system developed at the University of Waterloo.[19]

It should be pointed out here that computers were used for listing the chronological order of new words in 1970 by T. Finkenstaedt, Ernst Leisi and Dieter Wolff.[20]

Concordances, frequency studies, corpus linguistics

Computers were used for making concordances and frequency studies as early as the 1950's and 60's. For computational linguistics, H. Kucera's and

W.N. Francis's frequency studies were pioneering in the 1960's.[21] Of notable concordances of historical texts, the Shakespeare concordances should be mentioned.[22]

The Brown University Corpus of Present-Day American English consisting of c. 1 million words, was the first major machine-readable corpus made available to scholars (1964). It was later followed by the Lancaster Corpus, known as the LOB Corpus (the Lancaster-Oslo-Bergen Corpus of British English). These corpora have triggered a variety of linguistic studies often presented at the yearly conferences of corpus linguistics.[23]

Besides these two pioneering corpora of American and British English texts, the following English corpora could be mentioned:

1. The London-Lund Corpus of spoken British English, based on the Survey of Spoken English, collected at University College, London. See Svartvik, J. and Quirk, R., eds., *A Corpus of English Conversation, Lund Studies in English*, 56 (1980).

2. The Birmingham Collection of English Text of both British and American English written as well as spoken. The main text corpus comprises c. 20 million words and the corpus of specialized texts another 20 million words.

The extensive lexical research at the University of Birmingham under the leadership of John M. Sinclair, has led to the publication of the *Collins COBUILD English Language Dictionary*. It has also led to other dictionaries and lexical work and the project team has also extensive plans for future work in lexicography, grammar, the production of English language learning, material, etc. A special view of the work behind *COBUILD* was published in 1987, named *Looking*

Up An Account of the COBUILD Project in lexical computing (ed. by J.M. Sinclair).

3. A new Oxford Corpus or British National Corpus has been planned in cooperation between Oxford University Press, Longman, University of Lancaster, Oxford University Computing Service, and the British Library. The aim is to produce a corpus of c. 100 million words.

4. A new International Corpus of English has been proposed by Sidney Greenbaum at University College, London. The idea is to establish 12 regional corpora (covering 14 countries) and three specialized corpora. Research teams have been organized for the regional corpora in Australia, Canada, East Africa, Hong Kong, India, Jamaica, New Zealand, Nigeria, Philippines, Singapore, Great Britain, and the U.S. See Greenbaum, S., 'The International Corpus of English', *ICAME Journal*, No. 14 (1990), 106-8.

5. The Oxford Text Archive, Oxford University Computing Service, is an extensive collection of electronic versions of texts in many languages, covering nearly a thousand titles.

A number of other text corpora will be listed in the Bibliography, under C. English text corpora. It is, however, worth mentioning here that there are also large amounts of text available through private companies, large official organizations, etc. Newspapers and periodicals are also increasingly available in on-line format. Very large corpora of different kinds are now being collected especially in the USA, Britain, and Canada.

For the historical linguist the Helsinki Corpus of English Texts is of considerable interest. This machine-readable corpus covers texts of Old English, Middle English and Early Middle English, as well as American

English and Scots. The project headed by Matti Rissanen is intended primarily for syntactic and lexical studies but other areas of research may be covered, too.[24] Recently, Merja Kytö published her dissertation, *Variation and Diachrony, with Early American English in Focus*, which is a historical study on the variations and development of CAN (COULD) vs. MAY (MIGHT) and SHALL (SHOULD) vs. WILL (WOULD).

L.T. Milic, Cleveland State University, has made a corpus of English prose texts, published in England during the period 1680-1780. Cf. Milic, L.T., *The Augustan Prose Sample*, 1986, and 'A New Historical Corpus', *ICAME Journal*, No. 14 (1990), 26-39. This new historical corpus, consisting of prose compositions by 120 authors of the period, is called the Century of Prose Corpus (COPC).

Some of the corpora mentioned above and others can be ordered in various formats through ICAME (The International Computer Archive of Modern English), Norwegian Computing Centre for the Humanities, University of Bergen, Norway. A survey of all existing machine-readable text corpora has been carried out by Lita Taylor and Geoffrey Leech, University of Lancaster. A list of these corpora can be ordered from ICAME. See also Johansson, S., *Computer Corpora in English Language Research* (1982).

Software tools, retrieval programs
As was mentioned at the beginning of this article, new media and new techniques have increased the possibilities of retrieving information from existing material or databases.

One of the best-known text analysis programs is the *Oxford Concordance Program*, which produces word-lists, indexes, and concordances. The micro-computer version is called Micro-OCP and has (like OCP) been developed by Susan Hockey at Oxford University Computing Service.

WordCruncher is a text-retrieval program which is designed for personal computers and can be used with a number of indexed texts or corpora. There is, e.g., an indexed version of the Brown University Corpus, which can be ordered from ICAME.

LDB (The Linguistics Database) from the University of Nijmegen is a tool for searching analysed texts.

Nowadays there are several sophisticated text-retrieval systems like BRS/Search from BRS Software Products, Latham, NY, and PAT from the Centre of the *New OED*, University of Waterloo, Waterloo, Ont., Canada.

Much more could have been said here about computational lexicography, speech analysis and lexicography[25], artificial intelligence, and new media of the future. From what has been presented above, it should, however, be sufficiently clear that the historical linguist has now access to materials and tools which would never have been envisaged only a decade ago.

NOTES

[1] See Weiner, in Bailey (1987), 31.
[2] Aitken, in Bailey (1987), p. 119 and Weiner, in Bailey (1987), 41.
[3] *Oxford English Dictionary on Compact Disc.* Oxford University Press and TriStar Publishing.
[4] Aitken, in Burchfield (1987), 95. The scheme is here reproduced by permission of Oxford University Press.
[5] *PMLA*, 47 (1932), 890.
[6] Published in 1986 for the *Dictionary of Old English* by the Pontifical Institute of Mediaeval Studies.
[7] For the early history of *MED*, see *MED, Plan and Bibliography* (1954), ix, ff.
[8] See *MED, Plan and Bibliography*, Supplement I (1984), iii.
[9] 'Early Modern English: *OED*, New *OED*, EMED', in Bailey (1987), 73.
[10] See Aitken in Bailey (1987), 98.
[11] See, for example, Zettersten, A., 'The aureate diction of William Dunbar', in *Essays Presented to Knud Schibsbye, Publications of the English Department of the University of Copenhagen* (1979).
[12] Cf. Cassidy, F.G., 'The *Oxford English Dictionary* and the *Dictionary of American Regional English*: Some Differences in Practise', in Bailey (1987), 24-25.
[13] *Op. cit.*, 28.
[14] See *DARE*, Introduction, 'The *DARE* Map and Regional Labels', xxii-xxxv, by Craig M. Carver.
[15] See Görlach, M., 'The Dictionary of Translated Varieties of Languages: English', in Hausmann, F.J. et al (1990), 1475-99.
[16] Viereck, W. in Kytö et al (1988), 267-78.
[17] See Ihalainen, O., 'Working with dialectal material stored in a dBase file' in Kytö, Ihalainen and Rissanen (1988), 137-44.

[18] 'Beyond the Concordance. Lotus and dBase as Text Analysis Tools', *Computers and the Humanities*, 23 (1989), 375-83.

[19] 'Report in a New OED Project: A Study of the History of New Words in the New OED', *Computers and the Humanities*, 23 (1989), 385-95.

[20] *A Chronological English Dictionary: Listing 80,000 Words in Order of their Earliest known Occurrance* (1970).

[21] See Kucera, H. and Francis, W.N., *Computational Analysis of Present-Day American English* (1967).

[22] Spevack, M., *A Complete and Systematic Concordance to the Works of Shakespeare*. Vols. I-IX (1968-80).

[23] See Meijs (1987), Kytö et al (1988), etc.

[24] Cf. Ihalainen, O., Kytö, M. and Rissanen, M., 'The Helsinki Corpus of English Texts: Diachronics and Dialectal Report on Work in Progress' in W. Meijs, ed. (1987), 21-32.

[25] See Zettersten, A. and Holdgaard, T., 'The Talking Dictionary - A Demonstration of Natural Sound to be used in Connection with Dictionaries and Databases'; in Hyldgaard-Jensen and Zettersten (1988), 243-8.

BIBLIOGRAPHY

A. Dictionaries

1. *Abbreviation key*

AHD	William Morris, ed. *The American Heritage Dictionary.* Boston: Houghton Mifflin Co., 1969.
AHD2	Margery S. Berube, ed. *The American Heritage Dictionary.* Second College Edition. Boston: Houghton Mifflin Co., 1982.
AND	Ramson, W.S., ed. *Australian National Dictionary.* Melbourne: Oxford University Press, 1988.
CDEL	Patrick Hanks, ed. *Collins Dictionary of the English Language.* London and Glasgow: Collins, 1979.
COBUILD	*Collins COBUILD English Language Dictionary.* London: Collins, 1987.
DA	Mitford M. Mathews, ed. *Dictionary of Americanisms on Historical Principles.* Chicago: University of Chicago Press, 1951.
DAC	Gerald Alfred Wilkes, ed. *A Dictionary of Australian Colloquialisms.* Sydney: Sydney University Press, 1978.
DAE	William A. Craigie and James R. Hulbert, eds. *A Dictionary of American English on Historical Principles.* Chicago: University of Chicago Press, 1944.
DAf	Gerard M. Dalgish, ed. *A Dictionary of Africanisms.* Westport, Conn.: Greenwood Press, 1982.
DARE	Frederic G. Cassidy, ed. *Dictionary of American*

	Regional English. Cambridge, Mass.: Belknap Press, 1985.
DBE	John A. Holm with Alison W. Shilling, eds. *Dictionary of Bahamian English*. Cold Spring, N.Y.: Lexik House, 1982.
DC	Walter S. Avis, ed. *A Dictionary of Canadianisms on Historical Principles*. Toronto: W.J. Gage, Ltd., 1967.
DCEU	Allsopp, R., ed. *Dictionary of Caribbean English and Usage* (forthcoming).
DJE	Frederic G. Cassidy and R.B. LePage, eds. *Dictionary of Jamaican English*. Cambridge: Cambridge University Press, 1980.
DNE	George Morley Story, W.J. Kirwin, and John D.A. Widdowson, eds. *Dictionary of Newfoundland English*. Toronto: University of Toronto Press, 1982.
DOE	*The Dictionary of Old English*. Toronto: The Dictionary of Old English Project Centre for Medieval Studies (forthcoming). Microfiche: D1.1-D1.3 (1986).
DOST	A.J. Aitken, ed. *A Dictionary of the Older Scottish Tongue*. Chicago: University of Chicago Press, 1933-.
DSAE	Jean Branford, ed. *A Dictionary of South African English*. Cape Town: Oxford University Press, 1980.
EDD	Joseph Wright, ed. *The English Dialect Dictionary*. London: H. Frowde, 1898-1905.
EMED	*The Early Modern English Dictionary*. Suspended.
LDCE	Paul Procter, ed. *Longman Dictionary of Contemporary English*. Harlow (Essex): Longman, 1978.

LLCE	Tom Macarthur, ed. *Longman Lexicon of Contemporary English*. Harlow, Essex: Longman, 1981.
LNUD	Paul Procter, ed. *Longman New Universal Dictionary*. Harlow (Essex): Longman, 1982.
MD	Arthur Delbridge, ed. *The Macquarie Dictionary*. McMahons Point, NSW: Macquarie Library Pty. Ltd., 1981.
MED	Hans Kurath, ed. *Middle English Dictionary*. Ann Arbor: Univer-sity of Michigan Press, 1956-.
MEMEM	Bailey, R., Robinson, J.L., and Downer, J.B., eds. *Michigan Early Modern English Materials*. Ann Arbor: University of Michigan, 1975.
NZD	H.W. Orsman, ed. *Heinemann New Zealand Dictionary*. Auckland: Heinemann Educational Books (NZ) Ltd., 1979.
OED	James A.H. Murray, ed. *The Oxford English Dictionary*. Oxford: Clarendon Press, 1933.
OEDS	Robert W. Burchfield, ed. *A Supplement to the Oxford English Dictionary*. Oxford: Clarendon Press, 1972-86.
RHD	Jess Stein, ed. *The Random House Dictionary of the English Language*. New York: Random House, 1983.
RIT	Robert L. Chapman, ed. *Roger's International Thesaurus*. New York: Thomas Y. Crowell, 1977.
SND	William Grant and David Murison, eds. *The Scottish National Dictionary*. Edinburgh: Scottish National Dictionary Association, 1931-1976.
SOED	Charles Talbot Onions, ed. *The Shorter Oxford English Dictionary*. Oxford: Clarendon Press, 1973.
WNCD9	Frederick C. Mish, ed. *Webster's Ninth New Collegiate Dictionary*. Springfield, Mass.: Merriam-

	Webster Inc., 1983.
WNID3	Phillip Babcock Gove, ed. *Webster's Third New International Dictionary of English Language.* Springfield: G. & C. Merriam, 1961, 1981.
WNWD3	Victoria Neufeldt and David B. Guralnik, eds. *Webster's New World Dictionary of American Language.* 3rd College Ed. Cleveland: Simon and Schuster, 1988.

2. *Other dictionaries*

Ayto, J.	*The Longman Register of New Words.* London: Longman, 1989
Barnhart, Clarence L. et al.	*The Barnhart Dictionary of New English.* London: Longman, 1973. *The Second Barnhart Dictionary of New English.* Bronxville, N.Y.: Barnhart/Harper and Row, 1980. *The Third Barnhart Dictionary of New English.* Bronxville, N.Y.: Barnhart/Harper and Row, 1990.
Finkenstaedt, T., Leisi, E., and Wolff, D.	*A Chronological English Dictionary: Listing 80,000 Words in Order of their earliest known Occurence.* Heidelberg: Carl Winter, 1970.
Healey, A. di Paolo and Venezky, R.L.	*A Microfiche Concordance to Old English. The List of Texts and Index of Editions. Publications of the Dictionary of Old English.* Toronto: Pontifical Institute of Mediaeval Studies, 1980.

Partridge, Eric   *A Dictionary of Slang and Unconventional English*. 8th ed. London: Routledge & Paul, 1984.

Venezky, R.L.   *A Microfiche Concordance to Old English. The High-Frequency Words. Publications of the Dictionary of Old English*.Toronto: Pontifical Institute of Mediaeval Studies, 1985.

Wentworth, H. and Flexner, S.   *A Dictionary of American Slang*. Revised and updated by R.L. Chapman and renamed *New Dictionary of American Slang*, New York: Harper and Row, 1986.

B. Databases, CD-ROM

Grolier, *The Electronic Encyclopedia*. A 20-volume encyclopedia on CD-ROM. Danbury, C.T., 1986.

Historical Thesaurus of English. A computerized database constructed by the Department of English Language, University of Glasgow.

Languages of the World. NTC's Comprehensive Dictionary of American idioms. CD-ROM, Updata; Bureau of Electronic Publishing.

Merriam-Webster Ninth New Collegiate Dictionary. Highlighted Data, Inc.

Oxford Advanced Learner's Dictionary of Current English. Machine-readable text.

Oxford English Dictionary on Compact Disc. Oxford: Oxford University Press; TriStar.

Shakespeare: an electronic edition, based on *William Shakespeare: The Complete Works,* edited by Stanley Wells and Gary Taylor for Oxford University Press.

Shakespeare Dictionary Database, developed by Joachim Neuhaus, University of Münster, Germany.

The Dictionary of American Regional English. Based on 2.5 million replies from 2,800 informants.

The Longman Dictionary of Contemporary English. Machine-Readable text.

C. English text corpora

1. The Brown University Corpus. Brown University, Providence.
2. The Lancaster-Oslo-Bergen Corpus. ICAME, Norwegian Computing Centre for the Humanities, Bergen.
3. The London-Lund Corpus of Spoken English. The Survey of Spoken English, Lund and the Survey of English Usage Corpus, London.
4. The Helsinki Corpus. Department of English, University of Helsinki, Helsinki.
5. The Century of Prose Corpus. Department of English, Cleveland State University, Cleveland.
6. The Birmingham University Corpus. Birmingham.
7. The new Oxford Corpus or British National Corpus. Oxford.
8. The International Corpus of English. University College London.

9. The Oxford Text Archive. Oxford University Computing Service, Oxford.
10. The Linguistic Database. English Department, University of Nijmegen.
11. Bell Communications Research Corpora. Bellcore, Morristown. NJ.
12. JDEST Corpus. English for Science and Technology. Jiao Tong University, Shanghai.
13. Melbourne-Surrey Corpus. Australian newspaper texts. Department of Linguistics, University of Surrey, Guildford.
14. Kolhapur Corpus of Indian English. English Department, Shivaji University, Kolhapur, India.

D. References

Bailey, R.W., ed.	*Dictionaries of English.* Ann Arbor: University of Michigan Press, 1987.
Bailey, R.W. and	*English as a World Language.* Ann Arbor:
Görlach, M., eds.	University of Michigan Press, 1982.
Benson, M., Benson, E., and Ilson, R., eds.	*Lexicographic Description of English.* Philadelphia: Benjamins Publishing House, 1986.
Burchfield, R., ed.	*Studies in Lexicography.* Oxford: Clarendon Press, 1987.
Caie, G. and Chesnutt, M., eds.	*Essays Presented to Knud Schibsbye.* Publications of the English Department, University of Copenhagen, Vol. 8. Copenhagen, 1979.
Desmarais, N., ed.	*CD-ROMs in Print 1991. An International Guide.* London: Meckler,

Garside, R., Leech, G. and Sampson, G., eds. *The Computational Analysis of English: Corpus-based Approach.* London: Longman, 1987.

Hartmann, R.R.K., ed. *Lexicography. Principles and Practice.* London: Academic Press, 1983.

Hausmann, F.J., et al, eds. *Wörterbücher-Dictionaries-Dictionnaires.* 2nd vol. Berlin: Walter de Gruyter, 1990.

Hjorth, Ebba et al., eds. *Descriptive Tools for Electronic Processing of Dictionary Data, Lexicographica, Series Maior* 20. Tübingen: Max Niemeyer, 1987.

Hyldgaard-Jensen, K. and Zettersten, A., eds. *Symposium on Lexicography IV. Proceedings of the Fourth International Symposium on Lexicography,* April 20-22, 1988. *Lexicographica, Series Maior* 26. Tübingen: Max Niemeyer, 1988.

Ilson, R., ed. *Lexicography. An emerging international profession.* Oxford: Manchester University Press, 1986.

Kucera, H. and Frances, W.N. *Computational Analysis of Present-Day American English.* Providence, Rhode Island, 1967.

Kytö, Merja *Variation and Diachrony, with Early American English in Focus.* Bamberg, 1991.

Kytö, M., Ihalainen, O., and Rissanen, M., eds. *Corpus Linguistics Hard and Soft. Proceedings of the Eighth International*

	Conference on English Language Research on Computerized Corpora. Amsterdam: Rodopi, 1988.
Lancashire, Jan, ed.	*The Humanities Computing Yearbook.* Oxford: Clarendon Press, 1991.
Landau, S.J.	*Dictionaries, The Art and Craft of Lexicography.* New York: Schribner, 1984.
McIntosh, A., Samuels, M.L. and Benskin, M.	*A Linguistic Atlas of Late Mediaeval English.* Aberdeen: Aberdeen University Press, 1988.
	Computers and the Humanities. Osprey, Florida: Paradigm Press.
	American Speech. Tuscaloosa, AL: The University of Alabama Press.
	Publications of the Language Association of America (PMLA). New York.
Meijs, W., ed.	*Corpus Linguistic and Beyond. Proceedings of the Seventh International Conference on English Language Research on Computerized Corpora.* Amsterdam: Rodopi, 1987.
Milic, L.T.	*The Augustan Prose Sample.* Cleveland State University: Department of English, 1986.
Schäfer, Jürgen	*Early Modern English Lexicography.* Oxford: Clarendon Press, 1989.
Sinclair, J.M.	*Looking Up. An Account of the COBUILD Project in Lexical*

Snell-Hornby, Mary, ed. *ZüriLEX '86 Proceedings.* Tübingen: A. Francke Verlag, 1988.

Spevack, M. *A Complete and Systematic Concordance to the Works of Shakespeare.* Vols. I-IX. Hildesheim: Georg Olms, 1968-80.

Standop, E. *Englische Wörterbücher unter der Lupe. Lexicographica, Series Maior 2,* Tübingen.

Svartvik, J. and Quirk, R., eds. *A Corpus of English Conversation. Lund Studies in English,* 56. Lund: Gleerup/Liber, 1980.

Taylor, Lita and Leech, Geoffrey *Lancaster Preliminary Survey of Machine-readable Language Corpora.* Lancaster: University of Lancaster, 1989.

Viereck, W., ed. *The Computer Developed Linguistic Atlas of England 1.* Tübingen: Max Niemeyer, 1991.

Zgusta, L., ed. *Theory and Method in Lexicography: Western and Non-Western Perspectives.* Columbia (South Carolina): Hornbeam Press, 1980.

ICAME Journal. International Computer Archive of Modern English. Bergen: Norwegian Com-puting Centre.

Dictionaries. Journal of the Dictionary Society of North America. Terre Haute, Indiana: The Dictionary Society of

North America.
World Dictionaries in Print 1983. A Guide to General and Subject Dictionaries in World Lan-guages. New York: R.R. Bowker Company, 1983.
Oxford University Computing Service Text Archive. Oxford, May 1991.